Tales of a Mad Mystic

*New Parables
To Amuse and Confuse
Seekers of Truth*

John the Methodist

Tales of a Mad Mystic

By John the Methodist

For more information visit
www.MadMystic.com

To Ed Turner
Who taught me the art of storytelling

Contents

The Ten Great Laws of Organized Religion

1. If a spiritual leader issues vivid commands for people to love one another and live in peace,
they will fight over how these commandments should be interpreted.

2. If people build a temple to remind them to worship God and only God,
they will forget about God and worship the temple.

3. If people set up rituals to remind them to worship God and only God,
they will forget about God and worship the rituals.

4. If any revelation is so sacred that people preserve it word for word,
they will remember the words but change their meaning.

5. The more obvious and true spiritual teachings are, the more forcibly people will resist them.
The most clear, concise, and accurate spiritual leaders we call martyrs.

6. The more obvious and true spiritual teachings are,
the more creative people will become in their
misinterpretations.

7. If a spiritual leader insists he or she is only human,
people will insist he or she is from God.
If a spiritual leader insists he or she is from God
people will insist he or she is a charlatan.

8. Violent crime will always exist,
but large-scale atrocities require religious fervor.

9. People will resist the teachings of a spiritual leader who
strives to advance them
until another spiritual leader arrives to advance them
further.
Only then will they quote the former prophet to resist the
teachings of the new.

10. If a prophet reveals divine laws to liberate people
and keep them free,
it will only be a matter of time before these laws are so
narrowly interpreted and rigidly enforced that
they will create the very problems they were designed
to solve.

Fabulae
Antiquae

Ancient Fables

The Lost Chapters
of the Book of Genesis

On the sixth day...
God said, Let us make man in our image, after our likeness:
and let them have dominion over the fish of the sea, and over
the fowl of the air, and over the cattle, and over all the earth,
and over every creeping thing that creepeth upon the earth. So
God created man in his own image, in the image of God
created he him; male and female created he them. And God
saw every thing that he had made, and, behold, it was very
good. And the evening and the morning were the sixth day.

Genesis 1:26, 27, 31 KJV

On the 97th day, the Lord God came to visit the man in the garden he had created. He found Adam alone and spoke to him.

"Hast thou found contentment and is thy heart filled with gladness in this paradise I have created for thee?"

"Paradise? HAH!" said Adam. "I want my rib back."

God nodded.

"Trouble with the woman?" he asked.

Adam tried to speak, but only a series of growls and squeaks emerged. He pulled the hair on either side of his head.

"You seemed to like her when I first made her for you," said God.

"Yes, I did. She was so beautiful I just stood there in awe. You asked me what we should call her kind and I just said, 'Whoa! Man!' But since then things have gone bad... I mean REALLY bad."

"What's the problem?"

"She gets all upset with me, but she won't tell me why. She just expects me to read her mind, I guess. I ask her what's wrong and she says 'NOTHING.', but then she starts making all these little sarcastic jabs at me so I know there is too something wrong. She never notices the good things I do...only the mistakes I make. She's always cutting me down."

"She won't do anything I ask her to do," continued Adam. "I thought she was supposed to be my helper."

"Do you want me to destroy her?" asked God.

"Oh, no....don't do that. I like some things about her too. She is sweet sometimes. When she tells me how big and strong I am and how much she loves me it makes me feel so happy I feel like I'm in paradise."

"That's what I intended," said God. "What would you like me to do?"

"Make her show me some respect. Make her trust me. Have her just say what's on her mind instead of playing games with me."

"I know your needs before you ask," said God. "So I already created you with the ability to solve this problem yourself."

"How?"

"I gave you dominion over all the creatures of Earth. Can you guess why, Adam?"

"I've often wondered," said Adam. "I mean...I don't have the strength or size of the elephant, I don't have sharp claws like the tiger...why did you put me in charge?"

"Sometimes I wonder myself," said God. "It's your *intelligence*, Adam. You are far more intelligent than all the other animals. I gave you a brain. Use it. Intelligence can be far more powerful than the strength of the elephant or the claws of a tiger if you use it wisely. You should be able to figure out what the problem is with the woman and solve it yourself."

"Yeah, I am pretty smart now that I think about it," said Adam. "I'll see what I can do."

So, the Lord watched Adam go to the woman, and saw the woman throw sticks at the man, and behold it was not good. And the evening and the morning were the 97th day.

On the 123rd day, the Lord again found Adam alone.

"How are things in paradise?" God asked.

"I tried what you asked and it didn't work," he replied. "It's worse now than ever."

"What happened?" asked God.

"I used my brain. I thought...*what do I want?* That was easy. I want Eve to respect me. I want her to do what I ask. Then I thought...hey, I'm bigger and stronger. If I want Eve to do something I can MAKE her do it."

God grimaced. "Did it work?"

"Well, I had to be firm with her, but she did eventually comply with what I demanded... basically."

"Basically?"

"She obeys my commands literally, but you can tell she's not happy about it and if there is any way to thwart my commands without literally breaking, them she does."

"If I demand that she say she respects me, and if I'm forceful about it, she will do it, but it's just a joke because you can see she doesn't mean it. It's easy to get her to fear me, but I can't get her to love me."

"What if I made the woman bigger and stronger?" said God. "Would you obey her?"

"No woman is going to tell me what to do!" said Adam.

"But if she was bigger and stronger she could MAKE you do what you wanted."

"Maybe with my actions...but not in my heart.   I'd never let her control me."

"Hmmmm," said God, "Do you think something similar could be happening with Eve?"

Adam was speechless.

And it was good.

And the evening and the morning were the 127th day.

On the 247th day, God found the woman alone in the garden.

"What are you doing, Eve?" asked God.

"I'm preparing a feast," she said.

"Did Adam command you to do it?"

"No."

"Then why are you doing it?"

"Adam loves it when I do this, and he's been so nice to me lately... it just makes me feel good to see him happy. Thank you for having that little talk with him."

"And have you figured out what *you* need to do?"

"It took some time, but, yes. If I show Adam respect, he makes a real effort to make me happy too. I also can see that his brain works differently from mine. He can't know my thoughts any more than I can know his. I just tell him what I want now."

"So he's not giving you commands anymore?"

"No. He searches all over to pick me the flowers I like, he tells me how much he loves me all the time, he does little things to help me whenever he can....and just the other day, he brought me that."

Eve pointed to a huge stone disk with a hole in the center.

"What is it?" asked God.

"It's called 'the wheel.' I can't find any use for it, but Adam thinks it's going to change the course of history. It's the thought that counts.   Adam gets all excited about his inventions. They're the most important things in the world to him so when he gives them to me, it shows how much he loves me."

A grating sound and footsteps announced Adam's arrival. He was dragging a small log with one arm and carrying a five-foot-long stick with his other hand.

"Hi, God" said Adam.

"Peace, my child," said God. "What are you carrying?"

Adam raised the log. "I call this an 'axel'" said Adam, "and it's one of my greatest inventions."

"What does it do?" asked Eve.

"It goes with the wheel."

"Oh, I see," she said. She smiled and winked at God.

"This may not look like much now," said Adam, "but wait until I hook this up with my next invention. It's a little harder to figure out, but I'm going to call it, the 'internal combustion engine.'"

"You may have to wait a few years on that one," said God.

"Why do you have that small axel in your other hand?" asked Eve.

"It's not an axel, silly...it's a whole 'nother invention. It helps you when you are going on a long walk. It keeps your balance and it's useful for all kinds of things. I call it, 'the cane.'"

"CANE," said Eve. "What a nice name."

"How are things with Eve, Adam?" asked God.

"Eve's not such a bad person once you get to *know* her," Adam said with a smile.

Eve blushed.

Adam wrapped his arms around Eve. "You really outdid yourself when you created this one," Adam said.

And it was very good.

And the evening and the morning were the 247th day.

On the 2,158[th] day, the Lord God again appeared in the Garden.

"What have you been up to Adam?" he said.

Adam flashed a sinister smile. "Raising Cain," he said.

"Oh, Adam," said Eve. "He means our son, Cain, of course. Little Abel is becoming more than we can handle now, too."

"I swear one of those kids is going to get killed the way they fight all the time," said Adam. "They disobey the rules we only set to protect them, they always blame someone else for the wrong they do, they try to lie to us...you have no idea how it hurts to have your own children treat you that way."

"Do you want me to destroy them?" asked God.

"No, don't do that," said Eve.

"Don't try pulling that on me, again, God," said Adam. "I know you don't work that way. You're just trying to get me to realize how much I love them, and you succeeded as you always do."

Adam looked down for a moment. "I'm sorry I said you had no idea how it feels. I guess we're like your children, and we haven't always been obedient either, have we?"

"Seems like I do recall a little incident with some forbidden fruit," said God.

"You must teach your children how to get along, just as you two learned to get along. It is not an easy lesson to learn, but if you fail to learn it there is no peace. Future generations will fight and wage war and unspeakable evil will result if your descendants do not learn to love."

Eve looked thoughtful. "Is that why you gave us children in the first place?" Eve asked. "So we could see from your perspective?"

God smiled.

And it was good.

And the evening and the morning were the 2,158[th] day.

Paper Heroes

Leonidas noticed the first signs of battle three miles into the enemy's territory. It was as though a tornado had struck. By the light of his torch, he could see the bodies of the marauders who had invaded his land strewn everywhere on either side of the road. Carts were overturned, horses slain, nearly everyone was dead except for of a few wounded survivors who screamed in terror when they saw his Spartan uniform.

The raiders had attacked a border village hoping to pillage, plunder, and retreat quickly before defenders could arrive. They had destroyed the village and were returning to the safety of their home city, but it now seemed doubtful any would return.

More bodies lay along the roadside as he approached the enemy city. Leonidas stopped to examine several victims. The trademark wounds were unmistakable: the same warrior had killed them all.

Suddenly, Leonidas heard screams in the distance and the clanging of metal on metal. After he ran through a grove of trees, Leonidas could see a group of heavily armed soldiers lying dead or dying at the feet of one huge Spartan. The man had a torch in one hand, a sword in the other, and as he stood in the flickering light he looked like a demon from the lowest pit of hell. It was Karthos.

"Leonidas," he said, "what brings you here?"

"The commander sent me to help you capture the city," he replied.

"That's nonsense," replied the warrior. "He knows that I can take it by myself."

"No one doubts that, Karthos, but I convinced the commander that others should share in the fun."

Karthos grumbled his acceptance.

The two soldiers approached the city. A huge wall surrounded it. Hundreds of guards stood on top of the wall with torches in their hands, making a ring of fire around the city.

"Citizens of Havalinth," shouted Karthos. "I am Karthos of the Royal Spartan Army. My friend, Leonidas, and I have come to repay you for your crimes against humanity. If you surrender, turn over your weapons, and agree to serve Sparta as slaves, we will spare you your lives. If not, you will force us to kill you."

"I am Malinius, Lord of the city of Havalinth," a voice replied. "If you are foolish enough to attack us, you will die. We are not afraid."

Karthos rattled his blade in its scabbard and instantly the ring of fire disappeared as all the soldiers ran to hide. The Spartans laughed.

A huge log lay within a stone's throw of them. "Come on," said Karthos, "we can use that as a battering ram."

"Are you kidding?" said Leonidas. "That log must weigh a ton. It would take a dozen men to lift it."

"Hey," said Karthos, "It's us!"

The two huge warriors braced themselves beside the vast, gnarled monstrosity of a log. Their muscles tensed like knots of gleaming bronze and the massive log lifted into the air.

"There must be at least a thousand warriors in the city," grunted Leonidas, "...you sure we can take them?"

"My sword can slay ten thousand!" said Karthos.

"You pansy!" said Leonidas, "You've got to use a sword?"

The warriors began slowly, but gradually picked up speed as they approached the huge wooden gate. At the moment of impact, they moved with the mass and velocity of a speeding locomotive. A thunderous concussion and the sound of splintering wood came first, followed a second later by the thud of the dropping log and the clatter of wood fragments falling to the ground. Next came the terrified screams of the city dwellers as Karthos and Leonidas ran into the city with their swords drawn.

On they moved like well-oiled machines of massacre. Their blades swooshed through the air, slowing only slightly as they connected with human flesh. Their carefully orchestrated moves seemed like a captivating dance of death. It appeared darkly beautiful, causing their mesmerized foes to gape blindly at the terrible destruction that came to them. The Spartans were men with a mission. They did their work like the professionals they were. There was no hint of an expression on either face, except for of an occasional yawn from Karthos.

At last, they carved a path to the dark temple in the middle of the city. The black robed priests fell as easily as any other foe, but as they stepped inside the huge building each was overcome by a sense of profound evil.

Suddenly, there was a flash at the top of a black marble staircase. A manlike creature with glowing red eyes appeared. He laughed, and as he did so flames sputtered from his mouth. He pointed his hand at Karthos and murmured something in an ancient tongue. His sword became a deadly viper ready to strike him.

Karthos threw the snake to the floor. "Great Caesar's ghost!" he said.

"Wait a minute," said Leonidas, "Why did you say that?"

"He just turned my sword into a snake! Why do you think?"

"No, no," said Leonidas, "I mean, why did you say 'Great Caesar's Ghost'"? For crying out loud, this is 480BC. Caesar hasn't even been born yet."

"Hah! You just did the same thing yourself," said Karthos, "Why are you saying this is 480***BC***? They didn't start dating years like that until the fourth century ***AD***."

"That's nothing," said Leonidas, "I've got an even bigger question, how come two Spartan warriors like us are speaking English instead of Dorian Greek?!"

Wicked laughter made each of the warriors spin around to face the Sorcerer. "You fools," he shouted, "haven't you figured it out yet? Haven't you ever wondered why the hundreds of arrows your enemies fire never hit you, while the ones you return at them always hit their mark? Haven't you ever wondered why you can have any woman you want and win every battle you enter?"

"Yeah," said Karthos, "I have kind of wondered about that."

"You're not real!" said the Sorcerer with a sinister grin, "You're just the protagonists in a short story. You're the figment of some sleepy writer's imagination as he faced a deadline late one night."

The two Spartans looked at each other in horror. "What does this mean?" said Leonidas.

"It means you were doomed from your very conception!" laughed the sorcerer. "It means that you are destined to win every battle without the slightest challenge. It means you can take whatever you want and do whatever you please and nothing can even begin to stop you. In other words, you will die of boredom and probably take an audience with you!"

"No!!!" screamed Karthos.

"It's true," said the sorcerer. "Would anyone watch sports if they knew their team would win every time without any trouble? Would anyone buy a puzzle they could solve instantly without effort? Would anyone buy a game they could win every time with ease? Can't you see, it's the struggle that keeps us alive. It's the struggle that gives us a sense of exhilaration. The greater the struggle, the greater the exhilaration. You foolishly thought that victory, rather than the struggle itself, was the key to happiness, but in truth, victory without a struggle is not a true victory at all. You, my friends, can never know defeat, so you can never experience true victory!"

Karthos screamed and fell to his knees.

"Wait a minute," snapped Leonidas, "You're defeating us right now. If what you say is true then it can't be true because we have indeed lost the most important battle there is."

"Yes," said the sorcerer, "but if what I said is not true, then you have won again and what I said is true."

"Yes," said Karthos rising to his feet, "but if what you said is true—"

"Silence!" shouted a commanding voice. Everyone turned to see a man with long hair and an angry expression. "This is getting silly and the whole point to this story is getting lost."

"Who are you?" asked the Sorcerer.

"I'm the writer of this story!" he snapped

"That's not fair!" said the Sorcerer. "Writer's can't appear in their own stories. It's self-indulgent. It's against all the norms and conventions of writing."

"You should talk!" the writer snapped, "You thought it was great when our protagonists here used twentieth century colloquialisms. I've broken every other rule of writing tonight. I might as well break this one."

"You...you can't do this!" shouted the Sorcerer.

"I'm the writer. I can do whatever I want! In fact, I'm getting annoyed by you, so I'm going to write you out of the rest of this story."

"You...you...y...." the Sorcerer disappeared in midsentence in a puff of black smoke.

The two Spartan warriors looked at the Writer in confusion. "Geez," said Leonidas, "you've never done this before."

"I'm sorry," he replied, "but I had to. This was supposed to be a parable. This story was supposed to have an important message to it, but the senseless humor was getting out of hand."

"Well," said Karthos, "what happens next?"

"Oh, come on," said the writer, "surely you're not that slow. I kept you two characters around for a purpose."

There was silence for a moment as the two warriors looked at each other in bewilderment.

"Oh," said Leonidas at last, "I'm supposed to ask you...I mean," (he cleared his throat) "What **IS** the meaning of this little story?"

"I thought you'd never ask," the Writer replied. "I gave up trying to make the story speak for itself so I decided to just come out and say it."

"Too many people try to run from their problems instead of facing them head on. They think they will be happy if they eliminate them. They lock themselves in their own safe, little world. They don't want to hear about wars or suffering or the problems of others. They dislike the uncomfortable feeling news like this gives them. They fail to realize that this very feeling is a call to them...a call, telling them to stand up for what they believe.... to fight to make things better. This is why they were created... and when they answer the call they start to live life to its fullest."

"There are men who face no problems, hear no unhappy news, and never have to worry about struggles, but you only find them in graves. Many pray to God to take away their problems so they can find happiness, but they fail to see that perhaps God has allowed them to have these problems so they will do something about them and in the process find the very happiness they were seeking."

"I threw you Spartans into the story to show the folly of always having easy victories. Not only does this happen only in fictional works, but if it could happen in real life it would not necessarily be good."

"OK...OK..." said Karthos, "We got your message, now are you just going to leave us in this short story forever?"

"How about giving us some real enemies?" said Leonidas excitedly. "Let's have some arrows that can hit us. Let's have some villains we can't just mow down with our swords."

The writer laughed. "I'll see what I can do."

Medieval Madness

The Bishop and the Beggar

Once upon a time in a far away land, the people had grown to rely on a wise, elderly bishop as their spiritual guide. When he died during a time of great turmoil, the people felt lost and frightened. The highest authorities in the church decided to appoint Thomas of Engleton to replace him. He came from one of the most prominent families in the empire. He had gone to the finest schools, and already he had a reputation for great wisdom and spirituality, due largely to the stories circulated by his prominent family. His wise decisions and enlightened teachings were legendary.

Thomas came from a distant land and had a difficult journey to the kingdom. When he crossed the border into his new homeland, peasant rebels attacked his party almost at once. Charles, the leader of his personal guards, stumbled into the new bishop's tent. His skin glistened with sweat and there was an open wound on one of his arms.

"Your Holiness," he said, "they've fallen back once more, but they're regrouping. They will attack again and we won't be able to escape them. There's just too many of them and we're down to just a handful of our own soldiers."

"Did you send the messengers to the King as I commanded?" asked the bishop.

"Of course," replied the soldier, "but the royal palace is a half day's journey. If our messengers get through...which I don't think they will...the King will send a force to rescue us, but by the time they get here we'll all be dead except for you."

"Yes, of course," replied the Bishop, "they wouldn't dare to kill a man of God."

The soldier laughed loudly, "You don't know about these rebels do you? They're convinced the church has become corrupt and that all you clerics are working for the devil. They'll kill us soldiers on the spot, but you..." the soldier smiled grimly and shook his head. "They'll torture you for a week or two before they hang you."

The bishop grew pale.

Thomas sat at a small table and poured himself a glass of wine, but before he could taste it another soldier entered the tent.

"Your Holiness," he said, "a peasant has just entered our camp. We thought he was a messenger from our adversaries, but we found that he is a stranger to this land. His crops failed, so he came here in search of food. He wants a hand-out."

The bishop slammed his hand on the table so hard that he nearly spilled the wine. "How dare you bother me with such a trivial matter at a time like this," he said. "Take that peasant and..."

Suddenly a sly smile came to the bishop's face. "Oh Lord," he breathed, "I knew Thou wouldst not forsake thy servant. My talents and abilities are of far greater value to you than those of this peasant."

"This peasant is a child of God, no less than you or I,"said the bishop to the soldier. "Send him in to see me and when I am done talking with him, let him leave our camp unmolested. After he leaves I am going to sleep and I do not wish to be disturbed for any reason...even if we are attacked. Do you understand?"

The soldier nodded. The commands mystified him, and yet he knew enough not to question the bishop. He left the tent and a moment later the dirty face of a peasant peered into the tent.

"Come in. Come in," said the bishop with a warm smile.

The peasant took a couple steps into the tent. His clothing was torn, filthy, and threadbare. He peered back at the opening of the tent as though he was wondering if he should run away.

"Welcome, welcome, my child," said the bishop. He moved to the nervous peasant, placed an arm around him, and led him to another chair by the table before he sat himself.

"I understand that you have been faced with adversity," he said.

"Aaaaa...no," said the peasant, "my crops failed."

"I see," said the bishop with a look of concern, "and you have come to my dwelling in search of alms or perhaps a respite from the pangs of your involuntary fast?"

"Well, actually, all I want is a few coins or maybe something to eat."

"Certainly, my child," said the bishop, and with that he took off the ring from his finger and handed it to the peasant.

The peasant stared at the glittering ring in his hand. He started to tremble. "You want me to have this?" he asked.

"Yes, I do."

"Wow!" said the peasant, "I can buy food for my whole village with this!"

"There's more," said the bishop. "I want you to have this robe that I'm wearing, and the tunic underneath. They are made of the finest fabric and will bring you nearly as much money as the ring."

The peasant laughed. "Gee, you're really nice, Mr.....er, I mean Sir...or Father...or....what am I supposed to call you? I can never remember that stuff."

The bishop laughed. "You may call me Thomas," he said. "I would like to ask only one small favor of you in return."

"Sure. What is it?"

"When I give you my tunic and my robe, I will have nothing to wear. I would like to have the rags... I mean 'clothing' ...that you are wearing."

Within a moment, the two men had changed garments. It took the bishop a few moments to gain a tolerance for the stench, but when he had, he offered the peasant a meal of poultry, cheeses, sweet fruits and lots and lots of wine. Finally, he led the intoxicated peasant over to his bed where he stretched out and fell fast asleep. The Bishop, however, pulled his tattered hat over his eyes and shuffled away from his camp as silently as possible. Mere moments after he crossed the crest of a nearby hill he heard the sounds of battle as the rebel peasants attacked his camp for the final time.

ii

Twenty years after the attack on Thomas the Bishop, a multitude gathered for his funeral. Nobility from kingdoms in every part of the empire, and even beyond, filled his cathedral. Outside the cathedral, peasants, also wishing to pay their last respects, jammed the streets. Even the emperor himself had come to the funeral. He sat beside the king at the front of the cathedral with several of the bishop's closest disciples.

"Thomas was indeed a legend," said the emperor. "I heard reports of his wisdom almost daily."

"Having such a man of God in my domain was a great blessing," said the king. "My soldiers rescued him from the brink of death when he entered my kingdom. Peasant rebels had killed all his men and were preparing to do so to him when we arrived. His abduction had disoriented him a bit, but he sensed at once the gravity of the rebellion in our kingdom. He locked himself in his chamber and refused to eat or drink anything for three days. I can only imagine the fervent prayers he must have been saying. We tried repeatedly to get him to speak with our nobility, to give them advice and encouragement, but he knew where his priorities lay.

"Finally, on the Lord's Day he agreed to speak. He started to enter the cathedral, but then he turned back, refusing to stand before the people. After much coaxing, he started again, only to turn away again at the last moment. The nobility waited for him for three hours knowing that he had profound wisdom from the Lord to share with them. At last, they cried out his name over and over, begging him to address them. The bishop ascended into the pulpit, but only with the help of three other clerics who pushed him there. He looked out across the multitudes in the cathedral and wept.

"'It's all a mistake!' he cried, 'I am but the lowest of peasants! I am but your servant!' and with that he fell at the foot of the altar, crying out to God to have mercy.

"I can't tell you how moved we were," the king continued. "It wasn't an act. The tears were real. We had never seen such sincere humility. We knew the family he had come from, we knew the schools where he had studied, and yet, if you didn't know better, you'd swear that indeed it was just a frightened peasant who stood before us.

"When he learned the peasant rebellion was threatening to throw our entire kingdom into chaos, he insisted on speaking with the leaders of the rebellion himself. He went to the meeting alone and unarmed. In front of the rebels, he threw down his vestments and ring and declared that he was one of them. The rebel leaders were so moved by his courage, love, and humility they dropped their weapons and bowed before him, vowing to serve him as their leader.

"There was much rejoicing among the rebels that night. He ate with them and drank with them. He seemed to speak their language, even though he was wiser than us all.

"What could I do but do as the peasant leaders had done? I could see the hand of the Almighty directing his life so clearly. The peasants and the nobility began to work as allies instead of as enemies. And the bishop, true to his word, dressed in the clothes of a simple peasant, slept in a small hut and continued to confound us with his wisdom.

"People began to come from all parts of the world to hear him speak. He spoke with such passion and conviction. Sometimes his words were harsh and painful, but always they were right on the mark. I remember one time he shouted at a crowd that he was not a bishop, that he was no different from any of them.

"'You're all fools!' he shouted, 'why do you hang on my every word? I'm just a peasant! Seek God yourselves! Don't come to me. Don't ask me to give you the answers; I don't even understand the questions.'

"'Such wisdom.' murmured the people, 'and such humility. Tell us more! Tell us more!'

"'Leave me alone!' he cried. 'Think for yourselves!'

"'Yes, yes!' shouted the people, 'we will think for ourselves. Tell us more!'

After about a year, he began to ask young clerics to come to him and read to him from the Holy Scriptures. When they had finished, he would ask them what they thought the passage meant. As they told him, he would smile and nod and usually without even so much as a word from him, just by his expression, they could see their own folly. They would look deeper into the passage and discover truths that they had never realized.

"One young and foolish cleric asked him why he asked people to read the scriptures to him. He just smiled that familiar smile of his and said, 'I don't know how to read.' The people around him roared with laughter. He had such a fine sense of humor.

"It will be a long time before there is another like him," the king continued. "People came thousands of miles to seek his advice.

"'What do you think God would have you do?' he would ask them. They would invariably say that they had no idea, but when he smiled, and they could see the answer was obvious to him, they thought again and as he guided them with leading questions and simple gestures, suddenly the answer would strike them. His answers were always so simple and yet so profound. People were astonished that even though God had placed the answer right in front of them, they had been unable to see it until the bishop directed them to look with their eyes of faith."

One of the bishop's disciples fought back a tear. His voice shook as he began to speak. "We often begged him to give us just a morsel of his wisdom," he said, "but he rarely would share any. He wanted us to find wisdom from the same source he had found it. He wanted us to turn directly to God. Yet, occasionally, he could not hold all that wisdom of his in. Something would slip out of his mouth that would set us thinking for days.

"'Those who sleep in barns,' he said, 'smell like cattle.'

"Isn't that incredible? We were all baffled by its meaning at first, until one of our older members got to thinking that, if we dwell among the worldly and let worldly thoughts frequent our minds, there will be an air of worldliness about us that will permeate all of our being, just like the stench of your surroundings can permeate your skin and hair.

"Another time he said, 'If you plant seeds; they will grow.' Or how about, 'A blind man cannot see where he is going.' One time he said, 'Floors of dirt do not need to be swept.' Dear Lord! Everything he said sounded so simple on the surface, it sounded like something an illiterate peasant would say, and yet when you take a moment to think about it, there was so much profound wisdom underneath that it set your head spinning.

"Some of them I still can't figure out. One time he said, 'Clover has three leaves...but so does poison ivy.' Obviously there's a message there about how evil can appear as good to those who fail to use discernment, but I think there's a deeper meaning as well. I think it has something to do with the trinity.

"Often his teaching contained truth on several levels all at the same time. He once said, 'Naked men should not wrestle with porcupines.' For the life of me, I still can't figure that one out. I'm sure the nakedness refers to vulnerability, and on some level I know that we shouldn't be aggressive when we're defenseless, but I just can't figure out what that porcupine stands for."

"Just a few days before his death," the disciple continued, "he said something that I may never understand.

"'Faith can work miracles,' he said, 'even when the miracle worker has none. People with faith will be healed even when their healer is a fraud. God answers all prayers, but it takes faith to open our eyes so that we can see those answers. God used my blindness to open the eyes of others, my ignorance to bring enlightenment, and God has honored my humility.'

"'At last God has opened even my eyes. It is the greatest blessing to have nothing and know that you have nothing. I was born the lowliest of peasants, but when I die it will be as the bishop God made.'"

They lowered the body of the beloved bishop into his grave, and his soul was committed to God. At once, the sky grew dark except for a single ray of light that spilled on the grave. A murmur of awe came from the crowd.

iii

Five days after the interment of the bishop, soldiers brought a struggling peasant before the king. He screamed and cursed as they dragged him into the throne room.

"Why have you brought me this man?" asked the king.

"We caught him in the act of stealing, Your Highness," said a soldier.

"What have you got to say for yourself?" asked the king.

"I have a right to steal!" shouted the peasant. "I live in filth and poverty while you noblemen live in splendor. I do the work while you get riches."

"Are you not penitent for your sin?" asked the king.

"Penitent? Hah!" cried the peasant, and he let loose with a string of obscenities. "Are you or your nobles penitent for the way you've treated me? For twenty years I've been trying to get you to listen to me, but they kick me away from their horses, they tell their guards to beat me, they look down over their noses at me and treat me like I'm a worthless animal. And why? Just because of the clothes that I wear and the money that I don't have. No one will listen to me!"

"Speak," said the king. "I'm listening."

"I'm Thomas of Engleton!" shouted the peasant. "I was appointed Bishop to this kingdom twenty years ago but there was some mix up and some worthless peasant took my place. You're all a bunch of blind fools! You followed that simpleton like he was a prophet of God!"

The King's nostrils flared and he glared at the peasant. He stood up in a way that made everyone in the room stop what they were doing.

"How dare you speak that way about the finest man of God I've ever known!" said the king. "Take this man away and execute him at once!"

iv

Today, Thomas of Engleton lies in an unmarked pauper's grave, but if you go to the kingdom in which he was buried, you will also find a cathedral built above the tomb of Saint Thomas, who people now lovingly call "the Peasant." His story still inspires those who come to his cathedral. His greatness was exceeded only by his humility.

The Reluctant Ruler

Young Prince Rua often ran into his father's private chambers. "Daddy, Daddy!" he shouted.

The king looked up from his tankard of ale. His nose was red and his eyes were bleary. "Shut up, kid," he said. "I've had a rough day. Get out of here and leave me alone."

Prince Rua turned away as his eyes filled with tears. His father was almost always like this.

As he grew older, Prince Rua learned that his father's temperament troubled others as well. Oh, they were cautious with their comments around the Crown Prince, but he could hear a touch of sarcasm in their praise for his father.

When he became a young man and understood the political situation of the kingdom, the prince would go out drinking with his companions and they would talk openly about all the foolish decisions the king had made. They all agreed that he was too soft on criminals, that he didn't care enough about his subjects, and that he was leaving their kingdom weak and open for an enemy attack. The prince dreamed of the day he would become king. He assured his friends that he would solve all of these problems.

At last the day came when he did become king. After the proper mourning period for his father, King Rua sat down on his throne to begin his rule.

Many people requested an audience with him. He needed to make a long list of decisions immediately. There was a backlog because of the change in leadership.

The royal prosecutor brought in a thief for trial. He explained they had caught the man red-handed stealing gold from a noble.

"Hang him," said the king, pleased to have chance to clamp down on crime.

"But, Your Highness," said the man, "surely you want people to know you have mercy for your subjects. Can't you at least listen to my side of the story?"

"Speak," Rua said.

"I confess. I robbed him," the thief said, "but my family and others like mine are starving. I lost a son last week and one of my daughters is fading fast. The noble who owns our land will only let us farm it if he gets most of the crops himself, which he in turn sells back to us. We do all the work and he just keeps getting richer and richer. Why? Because he was born wealthy, and I was born poor. Does that sound right to you?"

"No, it doesn't," said the king. "Set him free and let him keep the money he took."

The people in the throne room gasped. "But, Your Highness," said the prosecutor, "if you do that every peasant in the kingdom will begin robbing, your nobles will revolt against you, and the kingdom will fall apart."

"That's a good point," said the king.

"But you can't hang me for just trying to feed my family!" said the thief.

"That's a good point, too," said the king.

The king's chief adviser pointed to both the thief and the prosecutor. "They are suggesting opposite things; how can they both have a good point?"

"That's a good point, too," said the king.

Everyone in the court erupted in laughter.

The king turned red from embarrassment. "Get him out of here," he said. "I'll decide his case later."

The prosecutor left the room and returned with a woman who had murdered her husband.

"Hang her," said the king.

"But, Your Highness," said the woman, "my husband got drunk and beat me almost every night. He nearly killed our little boy, and I can't see out of one of my eyes because he struck me so hard. He was just too big for me to defend myself against, so, God forgive me, to save our children, I waited until he was asleep and killed him."

"Set her free," said the king.

"But, Your Highness," said the prosecutor, "if you set her free, everyone will say you coddle criminals."

"If you hang me," said the woman, "everyone will say that you have no mercy for your subjects."

The king stroked his beard and looked thoughtful. "What if I throw her in the dungeon?" he asked his adviser.

"Then people will say you coddle criminals AND you show no mercy to your subjects," he replied. "Also, consider that the woman has young children. What will we do with them? Should they suffer for their mother's crime? They will if we lock her up.

The king was silent for a long time. "Get her out of here," he said at last. "I'll decide later."

The king took a deep breath. "What's next?" he asked.

"We need to recruit more soldiers and build more weapons," said the Minister of Defense. "The kingdom to the east has been building up its forces, and I fear it is planning an invasion."

"But, Your Highness," said his adviser, "we have no money for such a thing. We'll have to raise taxes. The peasants are starving as it is. If you care for your subjects, you will not grant his request."

"If the enemy invades, they will kill the men, rape the women, and take everything they have. If you care for your subjects, you WILL increase the taxes."

"IF the enemy invades." said the adviser. "Perhaps they are building up their military because they're afraid of us. We just finished expanding our own forces a year ago. Perhaps if we build ours bigger now they will build theirs bigger still. And if we tax our peasants too much, there is always the chance that THEY will revolt, and that would be just as bad as an invasion."

Everyone looked to the king for his decision.

"I...I choose...I choose not to decide." said the king.

"Oh," said the Minister of Defense, "so you're siding with him."

"No," said the king, "I just said I WASN'T going to decide."

"Yes, but if you do nothing, we will have no money to build our troops."

Much later in the day the king sat in his private chambers. He had finished four tankards of ale and was starting his fifth. His nose was red. His eyes were bleary. Suddenly his young son ran into the room.

"Daddy, Daddy!" he shouted excitedly.

"Shut up kid," said the king, "I've had a rough day. Get out of here and leave me alone." As he said the words, he got a strange feeling of déjà vu.

The king's Minister of Defense entered the room. "Your Highness," he said, "may I remind you that you promised to grant several people an audience tonight?"

"No, you may NOT remind me. I don't want to make any more decisions tonight."

"Very well Your Highness, but I remind you, tomorrow you will still have to make the decisions you put off today, plus the ones from tonight, and most likely many new ones that are not even on your list yet.

"Are they easy ones this time?" slurred the king. "I want a few where there is a real clear bad guy and a real clear good guy. I want a murderer who killed someone for a few pieces of copper he didn't even need. I want a rapist who without provocation raped an innocent virgin. Why can't I just get something like that so I can hang someone and feel good about it?"

"Things rarely happen that way, Your Highness. You must watch out for two types of people: those who make things seem simple are either simple minded or else deliberately hiding facts to manipulate you. Others will make things so complicated you won't be able to understand what they are talking about. This also is a trick to manipulate you. There are rarely clear choices. You must always listen carefully to both sides and then decide even if the values of one exceed the values of other by the width of a single hair. Even the wisest make mistakes sometimes, but you have to learn to live with it."

"No, I don't!" shouted the king. "I don't want this job. Get someone else to make all these decisions."

"As you wish, your highness. Whom shall I-"

"AAARRRGGGGHHHHH!" shouted the king, "Don't tell me I have to decide that too!...I don't know!....You!...YOU do it!"

"But....Your Highness....I..."

"Don't 'but' me. I'm the king and I officially appoint you to be the new regent to rule in my place."

And so, King Rua abdicated the throne and appointed his defense minister, Attila, to rule all the Huns. Attila quickly began a purge to torture and kill all his enemies and rivals including, of course, the former king, and all the people from Central Asia to Central Europe lived miserably ever after.

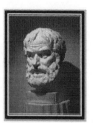

The Philosopher

The Rationalist

The Bard

Deleritus Profundus

The Scientist

The Methodist

The Pooh

Profound Madness

The Land of Light

Jeremy's rations had run out six days ago, or had it been two weeks? It was impossible to tell with no light to mark the passing of days. His hunger, aside from the maddening cravings now and then, had stopped. That was not a good sign. His body was starting to feed on itself. His metabolism had slowed. He felt lethargic and yet he feared going to sleep. He was afraid he wouldn't wake up.

Jeremy stopped beside an underground stream and refilled his water bottle. His plans for scientific discovery and adventure had certainly gone awry. His party had found the fabled caverns after a long search in the Amazon jungle, but in less than two hours a ledge had collapsed underneath them. The lengthy drop and the rockslide that followed had killed everyone else in his party.

At first, Jeremy considered himself lucky to have escaped with only minor bruises and cuts, but now he wasn't so sure. Maybe it would have been better if he had died instantly instead of slowly starving to death in the darkness of the cavern.

The darkness was unnerving. Only two flashlights had survived the fall, and their batteries had run out long ago. Jeremy now had to feel his way in the void, constantly dreading the possibility of falling into another crevice.

Jeremy was sure that madness had overtaken him when he heard the voices, but when he cried out to them, he could hear reactions. Within a moment, a group of people surrounded him, timidly touching him and murmuring in some unknown tongue. The people seemed as frightened by Jeremy as he was of them, but nevertheless they took his hand and led him through the darkness and Jeremy followed without hesitation.

They led Jeremy to what seemed like an underground dwelling. They offered him some food that he wolfed down quickly, even though it was far from appetizing.

Jeremy's newfound friends began to teach him how to navigate along paths they had made to keep themselves from stumbling in the darkness. As a good deal of time passed, he began to understand their language to some degree and could even communicate some simple requests. A few root words of their language were similar to those found in dialects of the Amazon basin. They seemed frightened by his questions about how to get to the surface. He was astonished to discover that their entire tribe had lived in the caverns for many generations, as far back as anyone could remember. None had seen light before and, in fact, they had no understanding of what "seeing" was.

Jeremy felt sorry for the kind people who had saved his life. They had never seen colors, forests, flowers, or waterfalls. They had never ventured beyond the small area of the cavern they knew so well. In unknown territory, they were vulnerable and they were afraid that they would stumble or fall.

Jeremy had a natural gift for linguistics. It didn't take long until he began to get a real handle on their language. He began to tell stories of his land, which he called "The Land of Light." His stories fascinated them but frightened them at the same time.

The elders said that their traditions spoke of a kingdom above, a beautiful land, which prophecy said they would return to one day, but they scoffed at the idea that Jeremy had come from there. The things he said about his land were not at all like their traditions.

Most were fascinated by the mysterious hair that grew on his face and by the way it curled. None had felt anything like it. He did not appear to be from their world.

The people loved Jeremy's music. He sang them songs from Aerosmith, Elvis Presley, and the group that quickly became their favorite: The Beatles.

They liked his stories, too, and soon large crowds began to gather to hear Jeremy tell them. It was easy to keep them entertained because they had never read a book, watched TV, listened to the radio, or gone to a movie. Jeremy told them all of the old "Star Trek" episodes and found they really liked the Batman stories he'd read as a child. Before long, his stories became so popular that people started naming their children Princess Leia and Bart Simpson.

Trying to translate the stories in ways they could understand was a real art form. It was surprising how many things could not be translated. One day, for example, a person asked him what he thought the most beautiful thing in his world was. After thinking for a while, Jeremy replied that he thought it would have to be a sunset.

"What is a sunset?" the person asked.

Jeremy explained that a sunset was like a painting made up of all different kinds of colored light. No two of them were ever alike, but all of them were beautiful.

"What is light?" asked one.

"What is color?" asked another.

Jeremy was dumbfounded. There was no way he could explain these concepts to these people unless they had experienced them. He tried to think of some word he could use, but it was hopeless. At last, he decided that he might be able to give them a slight feeling for what a sunset was like by using expressions they understood. He decided to compare it to sound.

"Light," said Jeremy, "is...like sound...I guess. There are many different pitches and timbres of sound. When we mix all kinds of different sounds into just the right order, we have music and it's beautiful. When we mix just the right colors and types of light together, we have a sunset and it is beautiful, too."

ii

The thing Jeremy missed the most about his homeland was the food. The people of the cavern had no spices or seasonings, and since they had no fires, everything was raw and cold. Their food consisted of four main things: raw bat meat, mushrooms, a fossilized plant material similar to peat, and the raw meat of some slimy fish that swam in their underground streams.

Jeremy frequently fantasized aloud about all his favorite foods, especially pancakes! Jeremy loved to talk about pancakes. He had such cravings for them that he dreamed about them when he slept. He tried to explain what pancakes were like. He told them that they were round, spongy disks covered with sweet syrup.

"What does 'sweet' mean?" someone asked.

Again, Jeremy was at a loss for words. None of them had ever tasted anything sweet. How could he possibly explain this to them? He had to let it go by saying that sweetness was unlike anything they had ever tasted.

One day, when Jeremy was talking about food, he thought he found something that they would understand: "cheese." They all knew what milk was because they had been fed on it when they were infants. Jeremy explained that cheese was simply fermented milk.

The groans and gagging that came from the crowd convinced Jeremy that this, too, was something that one had to experience to understand.

Everyone loved Jeremy's stories, but they often received them in a different way than he intended. Jeremy loved football and described it with great enthusiasm.

"We get the biggest men we can find," Jeremy explained, "and then someone kicks a ball to one of them and a dozen other men try to smash him to the ground. His team tries to stop them from doing this, so all the men start slamming into each other, headfirst, as hard as they can."

"You do this to criminals for punishment, right?" asked one of the people.

"No!" replied Jeremy, "We do it for fun."

The whole crowd of cavern dwellers roared with laughter.

Eventually, after more than a year of raw bat meat, Jeremy could stand it no longer. He announced that he was heading for the Land of Light and that he wanted to take his friends with him.

The elders of the people, who had long been jealous of Jeremy's popularity, were furious. They proclaimed loudly that Jeremy was a madman who was going to lead all his followers to their deaths. They told stories of horrible monsters and treacherous chasms beyond their land just waiting to swallow up the defenseless cavern people.

"Show us light!" said some of the elders to Jeremy, "Then we will believe you...then we will follow you."

"Follow me," said Jeremy, "and you will see all the light you want, but first you must trust me. You have to have faith."

The elders vowed that no one who left with Jeremy could ever return to the community, even if they discovered that Jeremy was wrong. This troubled Jeremy's friends deeply. If what he said was true, a much better world awaited them, but if what he said was wrong, it would mean they would lose everything.

Most of Jeremy's friends were afraid. At least in their own little world they were safe.

"Come with me," said Jeremy, "You will see sunsets, you will hear music, you will taste things better than anything you can imagine...you will be able to run in places you've never been to before without falling."

Yet, despite his pleading, when Jeremy left, only a dozen people went with him.

The way out was dangerous. Some fell into pits or stumbled and were badly hurt, but finally they saw a glow ahead of them.

Jeremy ran towards it. It was night outside, but the moonlight seemed as bright as a summer day after all his time in darkness. He laughed and danced, but then suddenly he noticed the others were terrified. They had no body/eye coordination. This new sensation confused them and made them stumble more than they did in the darkness. It seemed painful and frightening. One of his followers was so terrified that he ran back into the cave and was lost.

But Jeremy was patient with the others. He taught them how to use their eyes. It took weeks before they began to develop their new visual skills, and even then they preferred to travel at night, still relying mostly on their ears.

After two months, Jeremy and his friends made it to civilization. Jeremy immediately wired home for some money and threw a big celebration. He bought a large stereo system and played Beatles songs while he and his friends sat down to a meal of pancakes with lots and lots of sweet syrup.

iii

Jeremy and his friends became celebrities and earned much money through interviews, studies by anthropologists, and selling rights to their stories to the media. They lived well, but they never forgot the people they had left behind.

Within a year, they began searching for the caverns they had left, but they were in such a remote part of the jungle they had trouble finding them. They had to stop their quest several times to resume it at later dates.

On their seventh journey, 20 years later, they finally found what they were looking for.

This time they were prepared. They brought heavy-duty flashlights, battery operated digital recorders, even a battery operated digital video player. This time the cavern people would believe Jeremy.

Jeremy and his friends used no flashlights, as they wanted to get accustomed to moving about in the darkness and they didn't want to frighten the cave people. When they finally arrived in the cavern people's community, they found all of them congregating in a large clearing.

"Why are all of you here?" Jeremy asked one of the people.

"Don't be silly," the man replied. "We are here to watch the sunset."

This stunned Jeremy, but before he could comment, the man placed something in his hand.

"Here," he said. "Have a pancake."

The astonished Jeremy sniffed the so-called "pancake" and then tasted it. As far as he could tell, it was a round, spongy disk of the peat-like material they ate, but it was covered with some kind of mineral salt that gave it an acrid taste. It wasn't very palatable, but it was very special to these people who had never tasted any real seasonings.

"Who taught you about these pancakes?" Jeremy asked the man who had given him one.

"What is this?" the man replied, "Did you just run into a stalactite or something? Everyone knows the great prophet Jeremy taught us about pancakes many years ago. It wasn't until our high priest came along, though, that we actually got to taste them."

"Just what does this high priest ask for in return for his pancakes and sunsets?" Jeremy asked skeptically.

"He asks for nothing!" the man replied indignantly. "He risks his life for us and never asks for anything in return. When the Kingdom Above became evil, the Lord took away their blessings and gave them to us. Now we must be ever mindful not to become evil, or we will lose these blessings and be destroyed as they were. The evil one often tries to tempt us, but our high priest protects us."

"And you give him nothing in return?"

"He doesn't *ask* for anything, but it's only right to give him gifts."

"What kind of gifts?" asked Jeremy.

"We give him our most beautiful women," the man replied, "our best food, and all the servants he can use, and whenever people fall to the evil one and start talking against him we defend his honor... Just the other day we gave him a beautiful woman he wanted, and her husband became possessed by the evil one and started saying the high priest was a fraud... We executed that man this morning."

Suddenly the voice of an acolyte commanded everyone to bow before the high priest. The crowd became silent.

The high priest spoke in a deep solemn voice. "This is a story that was taught to me by the prophet Jeremy, who was, and is, and shall return someday to lead us once more."

The story was full of passionate shouting and frightening warnings of destruction for those who failed to obey the high priest. Jeremy couldn't remember ever saying anything remotely like it.

"Behold, the sunset!" shouted the high priest at last.

At once there was a horrible sound. As best Jeremy could tell in the darkness, the high priest and his acolytes were beating stalactites, swinging bullroarers and making strange vocal sounds. The resulting mixture was unlike anything he had ever heard.

Slowly Jeremy began to understand what was happening. The high priest was clever. He had capitalized on Jeremy's popularity by creating counterfeits of the things Jeremy had described. The "pancakes" certainly didn't taste sweet, but to someone who had never tasted anything sweet, they might pass as the real thing. Jeremy remembered that when he had tried to explain what a sunset was, he had likened it to sound. The high priest had taken him a little too literally, but to people who had never seen a sunset before, his forgery also could seem like the real thing.

"Your high priest is a liar!" shouted Jeremy when the clatter died down, "This is not a sunset. It's just a bunch of noise."

"That's blasphemy!" shouted the high priest. "How dare you blaspheme the teachings of Jeremy!"

"*I* am Jeremy, you fool! I have come to lead all these people into the Land of Light where they will see *real* sunsets."

The crowd murmured in astonishment. Some of the older people, including the high priest, recognized Jeremy's voice, but to most of the people, Jeremy's words were like those of a demon from Hell.

"I have given these people food from heaven," the high priest shouted. "I have shown them sunsets. What proof do you have that you are who you say you are?"

Jeremy had been holding back because he didn't want to frighten the people, but now he had no alternative. He grabbed his flashlight. "I'll show you real light!" he said.

When the light pierced the darkness there was bedlam. People shrieked with terror. Many were trampled as everyone ran in panic.

"It is the evil one, himself!" shouted the high priest. "Only he could do this. You must kill him at once or we will all be destroyed!"

Many of the bravest cavern people dutifully lunged at Jeremy and his small band. A savage battle ensued. The terrified cavern people killed Jeremy and his entire band as well as quite a few of their own people by mistake.

When the chaos finally died down, a small band of people realized that the real Jeremy had returned and had given his life to lead them to the Land of Light. They began to meet secretly to prepare for their own trip to his world.

The high priest commanded his followers to bring the belongings of Jeremy and his band to his private dwelling. Alone in the darkness, he examined each item carefully. Eventually, as he fondled the flashlight, he pushed the switch, which turned it on. After a moment of frantic fumbling, he figured out how to turn it back off.

There was silence for a long moment as the high priest waited for his heart to start beating again. Then he laughed long and deep. A sinister smile came to his face.

"This," he said, could be useful."

What if We're Wrong?

"Yahoo! Let's hear it for the Lions!"

Marcus grimaced as some cheap brew spilled down his back from the overexcited fan standing on the bench behind him. Why did they have to serve alcohol at the stadium? The hooligans and sports nuts were bad enough without it.

He glanced at his five-year-old son, Victor. He could scarcely see the action in the arena, but he held up his stuffed lion and growled just like many of the adults around him. He picked him up and put him on his shoulders so he could see better. This was almost emotional overload for the kid. He was clearly absorbing the excitement from the crowd around him.

Marcus glanced at his friend, Max. He was still just sitting there with his face in his hands.

"You all right, Max?" said Marcus.

"I'm fine," he replied.

"The food they sell here does terrible things to your stomach. Eat too much?"

"I feel fine."

"Looks like the home team is going to continue its winning streak, don't you think? I was worried when that one woman tried to kick the lion before it got her, but tough as she was, the lions are tougher."

Max didn't laugh. That wasn't a good sign.

After the ever-popular feeding of Christians to the lions would be the gladiator events. It would take a while to re-cage the lions and clear the grounds. Marcus bought some grapes for Vic to eat and then sat close to his friend.

"Something's wrong, Max. That's why I brought you here today. You used to love these things. I thought it would cheer you up."

"What's gotten into you? You used to be the biggest party animal I knew. We had to drag you out of the temple of Bacchus just before dawn, but over the last few weeks, you've started to change. What's going on?"

"Nothing," said Max.

"Come on, Max. I'm your best friend. You can level with me."

"I knew one of those Christians down there," said Max.

"Merda," said Marcus. "Did you know him well?"

"Her. She was the wife of a friend I work with. Sweetest woman you'd ever meet."

Marcus shook his head in disbelief. "Well, I'm sure she may have appeared that way on the outside, but those Christians are sick people. You know what they do at those secret meetings they have."

"It's not what you think," said Max.

"They're against the gods," said Marcus. "If their numbers grow, the gods will punish us. Our empire will crumble, and I've heard they drink blood and eat human flesh. They have this love feast where they do that and everyone has sex. I mean, they even let their wives go to these things. They're not like us."

"Ever talked with one?" asked Marcus.

"No," said Marcus, "and, by the gods, I hope I never meet one."

"You ought to some time. I've talked with a couple. They claim that they believe in only one god. They drink wine and call it the blood of their Lord and eat bread and call it his flesh. There is no cannibalism. They just think one god created us all and still cares about his creation. They believe that they can know him."

"I think they're feeding you lies to lure you in," said Marcus.

"I've been watching them," said Max. "I know who many of them are, now. They give to the poor. They help the sick. They have only two commandments: to love God, and to love other people. The ones I know follow that."

"Think about it," said Max. "We have a god of wine, a god of war, a god you can pray to when you lose something... For all I know, we've got a god of horse merda. Our gods fight with one another, cheat on their husbands and wives, they sound like we created them instead of the other way around. The one god of the Christians is strong, loving, and honorable, and the Christians seem to value these same things."

"Max," said Marcus, "You're starting to worry me. You sound like you're going to join them."

"Here's the big question;" said Max. "What if we're wrong? Have you ever stopped to consider that? I mean, what if there is just one God and they are worshipping him? What if we are laughing and cheering while men and women better than us are being eaten alive by lions in front of us?"

"All right," said Marcus, "Suppose what you say is right. There is just one god who loves us all and these Christians are following him. Why would a God like that allow his followers to die like that? Think about it. There are only a handful of them in the whole empire. Everyone else believes in the real gods. Do you think the God that created the entire universe would let that happen?"

"That's a good point," said Max. "He wouldn't do that, would he?

ii

Miles breathed a sigh of relief when he saw his wife, Rebecca. He should have known she'd be by the millstream. It was a peaceful place if you needed some time alone.

She glanced up at him as he approached. Her eyes were red from crying. He sat beside her.

"Did they do it?" she asked.

"I don't want to tell you, but, you'll find out one way or another-"

A loud sob cut him off. She knew what he was going to say. He placed an arm around her as she shook.

Tears flowed for some time before the shaking finally slowed.

"Both of them?" she asked.

"Yes."

"They were not witches," said Rebecca angrily. "He was the best teacher I ever had. He taught me about God. She used to invite me in for cookies whenever I went past her house when I was little. Everyone knows the Matherses were good Christians. How could they kill them?"

"We're not barbarians," said Miles. "This is the 16th century, for crying out loud. We didn't burn them without a fair trial first."

"What proof could there possibly be against them?"

"Hank Gibson testified that people were getting sick when they drank his milk, and it was fresh. He's a good farmer."

"That's stupid," said Rebecca, "It could have been something else."

"Well, there was eyewitness testimony that Mary turned herself into a cat."

"From whom?"

"That's not important."

"Just tell me."

"Well, it was Tom Chapman, but he swears he was sober when he saw it."

"He's a liar," said Rebecca, "How could anyone listen to him? He never liked the Matherses anyway. They reported him for stealing once and he always held a grudge against them."

"His testimony was not what did them in. It was their own words at the trial. Father William showed proof that they had been passing copies of the Holy Word of God translated in the common, vulgar language that everyone speaks. When the judge asked them if it was true, they admitted it. They said they wanted everyone to be able to read it."

Miles shook his head and took a deep breath. "Father William painted a vivid picture of the crazy ideas that would come if common, barely literate people started doing this. When he was finished, and if I hadn't seen this with my own eyes I wouldn't have believed it, Mathers stood and said that it could be no worse than the way well trained clerics had misinterpreted the Bible. He said that since they were professionals, they misinterpreted it professionally. Mathers claimed there was corruption in the Holy Church from the top to the bottom. He said that at times the church was more of a tool for Satan than for God."

"You really heard him say that?" asked Rebecca.

"I did. And they said other things even more shocking. They had been having their own little worship services, doing whatever they pleased without the consent of anyone in the church, even practicing the Eucharist and consecrating the elements by themselves. I couldn't believe their arrogance."

"I...I can't believe it..." Rebecca said. "But, I know you wouldn't lie to me."

Rebecca was silent for a long time, but finally she spoke. "Forgive me, Miles, but I have to ask this: What if we're wrong? I mean, what if what they are saying is correct? Mr. Mathers is a very wise man. We both know of clergy who have abused their power. What if this really is widespread? What if the Matherses were working for God and we just burned some innocent people to death?"

"I have to confess, the same thought has crossed my mind," said Miles. "But then I thought, would God allow corruption to be that widespread in his holy church? And if we believe that, would God allow his holy church to murder innocent people for speaking the truth? Only a handful of people believe like the Matherses, but millions of people believe as we do. Would God let that happen?"

"I...I guess you're right," said Rebecca. "I hadn't thought about it that way."

iii

Stan walked along the wharves gazing out at the ocean. It was clear day. He could see the sails of two ships in the distance.

"Stan? Stan Weaver?"

Stan turned to see Martin Jenkins. Beside him was a young boy.

"Martin?" asked Stan. "I don't think I've seen you since school. Is this your son?"

"This is my boy, Kevin. Looks just like the old man doesn't he?"

They both laughed.

"What have you been up to? What brings you here?" Stan asked.

"I have a plantation now, and business is good. I came because I told Kevin that when he was 7 years old I'd take him to the city so we could buy him his own nigger."

"I...I...don't know if that's such a good idea..."

"Don't worry, Stan. They have them cleaned up and fattened up pretty good by the time they put them on the auction block. I know you work close to the ships that bring them in.... believe me I won't let Kevin see that."

"I suppose you have to buy a lot of them for your plantation," said Stan.

"Last count 63."

"Do they try to escape or anything?"

"Hardly ever. They've got it better working for me than they ever had it in those jungles they used to live in. 'Course, I have to show them how to do almost everything.

They aren't too bright. Smarter than cows or horses, but not by much. They need civilized people to keep them from acting like a bunch of savages."

"Do you ever have to, you know, beat them?"

Martin Laughed loudly. "You've been listening to those abolitionists, haven't you? Whoo boy, the stories they tell! They'd have you believe we were standing over them with whips all day long. It ain't like that at all. We hardly ever have to beat one of them. You just do it for extreme cases and let the others see it, then you just remind them about it. Scares the hell out of them. They'll do whatever you say."

"Why would we beat them?" Martin continued. "We want them to be healthy so they can work. We don't want them nursing wounds for a few days."

Martin motioned for him to continue walking. He was going the same way.

"I don't know," said Stan. "I guess... it's just that my work is getting to me. I have to help unload the slave ships sometimes. I can't take that stench for an hour, and they pack those slaves there, like sardines, for weeks at a time. First, we have to take out a few dead ones. Some of the rest of them try to fight us and, Lord, the people on those ships are rough with them. Last week there was one with a dead child and she was moaning and crying. It was just like a white woman would do. And sometimes I can't help but ask..."

"What?" asked Martin.

"What if we're wrong?" said Stan. "What if they are just like us except for the color of their skin? We'd think they were monsters if black people ever did something like this to us."

"They ain't like regular people," said Martin. "God made them to be slaves, says so in the Bible."

"I'm not so sure," said Stan. "Have you ever met Branson Smith?"

"I've heard the name," said Martin.

"He's got this huge plantation south of here. His business is thriving. He bought 60 horses in one day here. I sold him some tack once. There's something wrong with the guy. You can tell the minute you talk with him. He's as slow as they come. He had this slave with him who explained what he needed, counted the money, and took the change. I honestly don't think Smith can even read, but his plantation is doing better than almost anyone else's. Rumor has it that it's because he has a slave who makes all the decisions for him. This slave keeps the books and runs the business. Some claim there are several slaves on that plantation that can read."

Martin snorted. "Yeah, yeah..." he said. "I've heard stories like that before. You can read them in some of those trashy papers right beside stories about women who are as smart as men and scientists who are working on flying machines. And I believe them just about as much."

"There has always been slavery," Martin said. "And there always will be. There's nothing in the Bible that says it's wrong. We've brought millions of slaves to this country. If God didn't want it, how come he lets it happen? And why hasn't the church cracked down on this if it's such a bad thing? You don't hear any preachers complaining about it. I mean, except for a few nut cases now and then. My preacher told me the Bible says slaves are supposed to obey their masters."

Martin thought about it. Should he follow his heart, the church or the predominance of public opinion?

What if we're wrong?

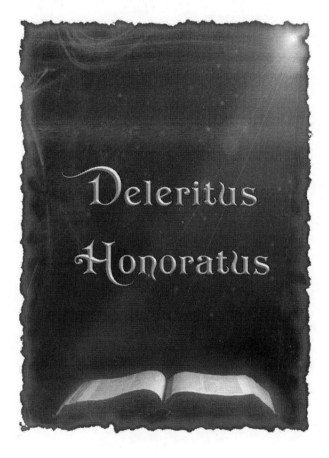

Deleritus

Honoratus

Respectful Madness

Heirlooms

October 3, 1993

Paul looked at the array of boxes on the floor of his living room. He felt like a mountain climber about to embark on a journey to the top of Mount Everest. The task ahead seemed impossible, and unlike a mountain climber there would be little exhilaration at the end of his quest. Sorting through dozens of boxes of old junk was scarcely as lofty a pastime as mountain climbing, but he had to do it. There was enough clutter in his apartment already. When he had picked up the boxes, his first impulse had been just to drive his borrowed pickup truck straight to the dump. Part of him still wished he had, but he couldn't just throw it out without at least looking at what he had acquired. He owed at least that much to his father.

After his father's death, they read the will. His sister, Martha, had gotten the house. His older brother, Stan, had received the certificates of deposit, the car, and all the investments. And last but not least? He, Paul Cassidy, had acquired all the things in Grandpa's room.

Paul laughed. How ironic. He knew that this was his father's way of telling him how much he loved him. The things in Grandpa's room were his most treasured possessions. The fact that they were now his was proof positive that, "Daddy always liked him best."

Paul mused that he wished he hadn't been so popular with his father. Then perhaps he could have gotten the investments.   His father's actions had touched him, nevertheless.

Paul could scarcely remember his grandfather, who had died when Paul was five years old, but he knew the man had been perfect. At least, that was the impression he'd gotten from hearing his father talk about him.

Apparently, others didn't feel that way. When he was seven, Paul spent the summer with his uncle and aunt who still lived near Grandpa's hometown of Maplecrest. When adults there heard the name "Cassidy," they invariably asked if he was the grandson of Joe Cassidy. There was likely a family resemblance that encouraged the question, as well. The first few times he had owned up to it proudly. Then, he noticed the strange reactions.   Sometimes they smiled and shook their head. Sometimes the smiles left their faces. Once an elderly woman had even crossed herself, which at seven had made him wonder if Grandpa was a werewolf or something similar.

He finally asked Aunt Mary why everyone treated him funny, and he could see that it opened some old wounds.

"It's probably best not to talk too much about your grandfather," she replied. "He was a good man, but he had some crazy ideas that no one understood. He wasn't the same after your grandmother died."

This made Paul reluctant to say his last name for the rest of the summer, but it also made him wonder about the rest of the story.

When he returned home, his father had an even stronger reaction than his aunt did. He seemed defensive. He immediately insisted that his father had been the best father ever. "People just don't understand," he said finally.

Paul remembered his grandfather's funeral. He'd never seen his father cry before that. It was scary to watch his father, who was talkative by nature, suddenly become silent for what seemed like months.

Even two years later, when he returned from Maplecrest and started to ask questions, the wound was still there. Paul thought it wise not to ask any more questions.

Then there was always "Grandpa's room." Dad had kept those boxes there, and the room was absolutely off limits to everyone. Naturally, curiosity had overcome him once, and this had earned him one of the few cases of corporal punishment he could remember from his father, a spanking followed by an angry lecture about respect.

The questions remained, and after his mother's stroke she said some strange things that only made things worse. Sometimes she was unresponsive after the stroke, other times she was delusional, but on her good days, she was almost like she had been before. She was like that one day when he stopped by to watch her while Dad did some shopping. Why his questions about Grandpa came out then, he had no idea.

"He liked children," she said, "They were the only ones who understood him. They spoke his language. Children gathered wherever he went. The things he said never upset them, like the adults. It's funny that children would relate to him like that with his background."

"What background?" Paul asked., but it was too late. She had spoken all she would that day. Her eyes lost their focus and her mouth stayed shut.

After his mother's death, his father had made a few more references that Paul vividly remembered.

Dad often got angry during elections.

"Look at what they're doing" he blurted once after a particularly nasty political ad appeared on television. "Guilt by association... negative speculation masquerading as fact... destroying a good man by playing on people's worst fears... Why do people always fear what they don't understand? Why do they have to destroy good people? They did that to your grandfather."

The next revelation came just after Paul had sold his first story to a magazine. "You get your writing ability from your grandfather, you know," Dad said. "He could have been famous if Mom hadn't died and he didn't have to spend all his time taking care of us."

Paul knew the basic facts. Grandma had died at the age of 36, leaving behind three children. His father had been 16 at the time. Aunt Mary was only 7. Grandpa had always been somewhat of a recluse, but after his wife's death, his public excursions were rare.

Writing ability: that much made sense. Paul noted that this was the one thing he remembered about his grandfather. He could tell some great stories. He remembered sitting by the fireplace with his brother and sister while Grandpa would tell about the monsters he'd had to fight when he was exploring the jungles of South America, or the time space aliens captured him and he narrowly managed to escape by overpowering one of their guards and firing a stolen ray gun into their central power unit.

And Grandpa could play. He remembered just after Christmas one year when Grandpa got to baby-sit. They pretended they were spies and hunted each other with dart guns that shot the old darts with rubber suction cups on the ends. Predictably, one of Grandpa's darts hit a vase and knocked it off a table, so they got into his car and went to Woolworth's to get another one to replace it.

Was this what his mother was referring too? The memories Paul still had made Grandpa appear like a big kid who had never grown up. But why would this upset adults? His speculation on this was disturbing, to say the least.

After Paul received his first book advance from a publisher, his father told him that Grandpa had pegged him as a writer before his fourth birthday. "He used to sit down with you for hours and listen to the stories that you would tell him," he said. "You were always his favorite."

When Dad got sick near the end and Paul's sister had suggested cleaning some of the junk out of the old room, Dad went nuts. He was furious that his daughter could even think of such a thing. Martha was a neat freak if there ever was one. She thought Dad was senile for behaving that way. She used to joke about "Saint Grandpa," as she used to call him. After the reading of the will, Martha wanted the things moved out of

Grandpa's room as quickly as possible. She already had plans to make the room into a playroom for her kids.

"Might as well get started," Paul muttered to himself.

He dreaded the work. Old papers filled most of the boxes; he could tell from the aches and pains he still felt from trying to carry them, but a few of the boxes were different. They looked like large cases for machinery or something. Paul decided to open one of them first.

Paul laughed when he opened it. It was a camera...an *ancient* camera...one of those huge monstrosities that you had to hide under a black hood to focus.

Paul mused that his grandfather had been like him in more ways than one. Not only did he have a flair for writing, but they also shared an interest in photography. As he thought about it, he remembered that Grandpa had had many photographs on the wall of his room. He could even remember posing with his brother and sister for some family portraits.

"Oh well," thought Paul, "I guess it's not a total loss. Some collector might pay a few bucks for an antique like this."

Paul opened the next box. He pulled out a large and heavy piece of equipment. It was another camera of some type, but unlike anything he'd ever seen. It had bellows on the front and a finely crafted steel box behind it. It was covered with knobs and dials to control its many functions. Along with the two cameras were several carefully designed cases with dozens of lenses, a few tripods, and a few boxes full of darkroom equipment.

The next day, Paul managed to squeeze all the equipment into his Chevy and drove them over to the local camera shop he frequented.

Mr. Maxwell, the owner of the store, did a lot of business selling used and antique equipment.

"Ever see one of these before?" said Paul. He grunted as he pulled the first camera out of its case and raised the huge piece of equipment to lay it on the counter.

Mr. Maxwell whistled. "Well, I'll be," he said, "That's a Wright/Hirkos 8x10 View camera. They were popular around the turn of the century for people who could afford them. Had some of the best lenses ever made. Too bad you haven't got any. They're worth a fortune."

Paul smiled and ran back out to his car. When he opened the next case he thought Mr. Maxwell's eyes were going to pop out of his head. He picked up the lenses one at a time and examined them carefully in the light. "My word!" said Mr. Maxwell, "these lenses are almost mint."

Mr. Maxwell paused and scowled for a moment. I suppose I shouldn't have acted so excited. You're probably expecting a pretty good price for these now aren't you?"

Paul laughed. He'd worked with Mr. Maxwell for years; he knew he wouldn't cheat him.

"How about this other camera?" asked Paul.

Mr. Maxwell took the other case and opened it. He stared at it for a long moment then glanced up at Paul.

"I...I can't believe this!" he said, and with that Mr. Maxwell went back into his office emerging a few moments later with a well-worn book. He quickly thumbed through the pages until he found what he was looking for and then glanced back into the case again.

"I've only seen one of these before in my whole life," said Maxwell at last. "If you have a full set of lenses for this one, I think I'll pass out."

Paul placed a few more cases on the counter and Maxwell gasped as he looked inside each one.

"What we have here," said Maxwell, "is a Serliflex. It's unlike any other camera ever made. A German firm invented it just about the same time the Second World War started. Their plant was destroyed by bombings before they could make many of these. They barely had time to get it beyond the prototype stage. It was decades ahead of its time. It used 4x5 sheet film but it had a finely crafted mechanism that allowed you to take 20 shots without reloading. To this day, no other camera company has been able to do that successfully. It was one of only a handful of cameras over the years in this format that used a reflex mirror to allow you to see through the lens before you took the picture. The optics in this baby are incredible. The prism used in the viewfinder alone is priceless, but the lenses are worth even more. And it's got all the tilt and shift functions of the finest view cameras as well. It's not just collectors who want these. If you find a professional photographer, they'd kill to get their hands on one. It was one of the most versatile and highest quality cameras ever constructed, and it's built to withstand anything short of a nuclear holocaust."

"What do you think it's worth?" asked Paul.

Mr. Maxwell laughed. "I don't mind telling you that it's more than I can afford. If I sold all the other cameras in this store, I couldn't afford to buy it. We're talking six figures, minimum."

Paul listened in awe as Mr. Maxwell described all the innovative features of his camera. It fascinated him just as he was sure it had fascinated his grandfather before him. At last, the temptation was just too great. He decided to take it home and try it out himself, but before he left, Mr. Maxwell gave him a check for $5,000 for the 8x10 view camera.

Several months passed before Paul had a chance to return to his cluttered living room to try to sort out the rest of his grandfather's belongings. He'd set up a darkroom and a photography studio like a man possessed. Already, he had contracts for more than $30,000 dollars based on the portfolio he had created in less than three weeks. This more than compensated the hefty insurance he had to pay on his equipment, which was valued at nearly a half million dollars. Just as Maxwell said, Paul's photographer friends tried everything to bribe him so they could play with his new toy just once.

As Paul looked at the endless array of boxes in front of him, he noticed that many of them were similar: 8 ½ by 1e1-

inch boxes constructed of a fine archival cardboard. Paul opened one and, as he had guessed, the box was filled with photographs. He sat down and began to examine them one at a time. They were all of the same subject, his grandmother. As Paul examined the photographs, he could see why his grandfather had developed such an interest in photography. *If I had a wife like that,* thought Paul, *I'd probably spend most of my time taking pictures of her, too.* She would have been breathtaking, even without the careful lighting and composition in the photos. Paul marveled at the artistic excellence in nearly every picture.

After several hours of looking at pictures, Paul began to examine some of the papers in the other boxes. The first box didn't surprise him at all. It was poetry, love poetry, written by his grandfather to his grandmother. Paul started reading the poetry and couldn't stop. He had majored in English Literature in college and yet, in all his years of study, he had never read anything as moving or as expressive as this. When sunlight started streaming in through the windows, Paul looked at the clock for the first time. He had been in his grandfather's world for nearly twelve hours and he hadn't even noticed the time.

Paul went to his telephone and canceled all his appointments. He put a couple of bagels in the microwave, fixed himself a cup of tea, and resumed his reading.

Almost a year later, Paul received a phone call from his agent. "Paul," she said excitedly, "your last book hit the best-seller list so fast they're willing to offer you a $500,000 advance for your next one. That's just an advance, mind you; your royalties could bring you a dozen times that much. The book of photographs and poetry isn't selling as well, but it's getting rave reviews from the critics. They're putting your grandfather in a class with Ansel Adams and T. S. Eliot. One review even compared him with Renaissance men like Michelangelo and Da Vinci."

"How many more stories have you got?" she asked.

"So far I've found about 200 short stories, 300 poems, and 6 novels."

"What do you mean, 'so far'?"

"I've still got a few boxes of his I haven't opened yet," replied Paul.

There was a long silence on the other end of the phone. When his agent resumed talking her voice was shaking. "Oh Paul," she said at last, "I wish you hadn't told me that. I'm not going to be able to sleep tonight."

The trips back to Maplecrest were inevitable. There was obviously much to learn about Grandpa. The older people invariably remembered him. Clearly, he had been the subject of much speculation and talk. Paul found diplomas for graduate degrees from Columbia in the boxes, and a few published articles that had won him some serious respect in his early years, but no one seemed to know about that. What nearly everyone did remember was that he had walked away from not just one or two, but *three* lucrative positions for no reason. At one time, he actually owned the local newspaper, but he sold it and then went into seclusion for a couple of years. No one knew what he did with all his money, but there was solid speculation that he had a gambling problem.

According to public opinion, he was deranged. Why else would a boy raised as a good Baptist start attending the local Congregational church and then leave that one for the Methodists, and then, merciful heavens, he even went to the Catholics and the godless Unitarians. In his later years, he seemed to pick churches at random, often going to a different church each week.

At first the churches welcomed him, always excited about a new member, but some of them had invited him to discussion groups where invariably he stirred up trouble. It wasn't that he was disrespectful, it was just the questions he kept asking and the weird ways he interpreted the Bible. He knew it backwards and forwards (mostly backwards, according to one Baptist woman), but he didn't seem to have the faith to accept it the way God meant it.

Apparently, there were still hard feelings because Grandpa, as a young man, used to take his wife out dancing. Dancing! He certainly had been raised better than that. His home church flat-out forbid this, but even the churches that didn't forbid it at least frowned on it in those days.

More memories filled his head after his talk with one particular church lady. In Paul's own church growing up there had been some controversy over the song "Lord of the Dance." It was based on an old Shaker melody. A Sunday School teacher had taught the song to the primary class, and this upset some parents who didn't feel the song was appropriate for church.

Martha used to love that song. She started singing it for Grandpa one time, and he took her arms and started dancing and singing right with her. Paul could remember Grandpa swinging her in the air and Martha laughing so hard she could hardly sing.

Some in Maplecrest were convinced Grandpa was a communist. He rarely spoke in public, but the few times he did he opposed removing leftist books from the public library, hiding behind First Amendment rights when he should have been standing behind his country, and he always seemed opposed to sending troops anywhere.

And the books he used to read! The local librarian had alerted the community that Grandpa was a dangerous man they should keep an eye on.

Paul found it odd that everyone seemed shocked when he told them of his Grandfather's service record. Paul knew the facts. He'd found the papers and medals in the boxes.

Grandpa had good reason to oppose the hasty deployment of troops.

Paul went to his new study. He punched in the numbers on the security lock and listened to the bolts snap open. It was always pleasant walking into this room. The temperature and humidity controls not only preserved his priceless collection of manuscripts but also made it comfortable.

Paul looked at the box on the floor in front of him. The last one.

At first he'd devoured his grandfather's material. He couldn't get enough of it. His friends thought he was nuts secluding himself in his house for days at a time to read, but after the first manuscript was edited and published, everyone understood.

After a while, Paul decided to ration his reading so he could make his enjoyment last for as long as possible. As Paul looked at the last box, he felt a twinge of sadness as he realized that it would all soon be over, but his sense of excitement overpowered the sadness easily as he removed the cover.

When Paul looked inside, his heart stopped. On the top of the collection of manuscripts was a letter. It opened with the words: "Dear Paul,"

Paul trembled as he pulled the letter out of the box and began reading.

"Dear Paul," said the letter, "You're only five years old at the time I'm writing this. My health is failing me, and I know I won't live to tell you the things I want to tell you. You're just too young to understand it all now. I want to thank you for all you've done for me. You've made this old man very happy. When I look in your eyes, I see myself looking back. Already in you I see that same sense of wonder, that same creativity, that same artistic sense that's always been a part of me. I know that someday you will be a great writer yourself. Already you've told me some of the most delightful stories I've ever heard. I wrote them all down so that you could read them when you got older, and I thought I'd share with you a few of mine as well. To some I'm sure my writings won't be worth much more than the paper they're written on, but, like my wife, I'm sure someone like you will find that they are worth more than gold.

I hope you enjoy my cameras; they meant a lot to me. And I hope you enjoy getting to know my wife. She was the most beautiful woman who ever lived, in more ways than one. I'm sorry you never met her in person, but perhaps you'll understand what I mean as you read what I wrote about her.

Most important of all, I hope you treasure my prized possession. I give this to you, my grandson, hoping that it will provide as much for you as it did to your grandmother and I. It's without a doubt the greatest masterpiece of all."

Paul was still shaking when he finished the letter. The prophetic words of his Grandfather were astonishing. He felt as though his Grandfather had just spoken to him from beyond the grave.

It was just as he had said. By reading his writings, he had come to know both his grandfather and grandmother as if they were his closest and dearest friends. The many letters they had written back and forth, the love poetry, the short stories and novels, they had all painted a picture of his grandfather's soul that had moved him more than anything in his life.

But what was this talk about his "prized possession?" Was it one of the magnificent books he'd already read, or was it some unspeakable treasure that lay hidden among the manuscripts he had yet to read? Paul carefully thumbed through the papers below the letters he'd just read. He laughed when he found a large stack of short stories that had been written by him!... Paul Cassidy. It was just as his grandfather had said. He'd listened to his little four-year-old grandson and written down all those stories.

Paul read the stories and laughed loudly. He couldn't remember writing them, but he could clearly distinguish his own personality traits coming out of the stories. It was a wonderful peek into the mind of a four-year-old.

After he finished reading the stories from his childhood, Paul continued to dig into the box. Near the bottom he found an intricate wooden box large enough to hold a good-sized manuscript. It was large enough for another novel. Was this the "prized possession" he'd read about?

As Paul opened the box, he felt as though he was making history. He could see himself telling others about this dramatic moment years later when he wrote his own autobiography, but as he looked into the box his heart sank. It was not a manuscript at all, but a large, commercially bound book.

There was a note on top of it.

"Dear Paul," it said, "This is my prized possession. I hope it means as much to you as it did for your grandmother and I."

Paul moved the paper. Beneath it was a tattered old Bible. He crashed back to reality as he realized his hope for another original manuscript had been for nothing.

It wasn't even a good Bible. It looked like a cheap one that you could buy in a five and dime store back in the 1930s.

Paul sighed deeply and stood for a moment. He looked at the stacks of paper in front of him and surveyed the archival cases filled with more writings around him. He laughed loudly as he remembered how he had almost taken the whole collection to the dump after his Mother's death. What an incredible waste that would have been, all those priceless treasures thrown away because he hadn't taken the time to look beyond their surface value.

Suddenly, Paul looked back at the old Bible. Was he about to make the very mistake he had just been thinking about? He picked up the old book and started thumbing through it. Little penciled in notes, scraps of paper, and special markings filled it.

Paul remembered how his grandfather had always wanted to take him to church as a child. He remembered his grandfather talking about Jesus. He'd explained to him that Jesus was his best friend. Paul hadn't had much time for religion since then, but now, for some reason, he felt compelled to sit down and start reading. He opened the Bible to Matthew.

When Paul saw sunlight streaming in through the windows, he looked at his clock for the first time. He had been lost in his *Father's* world for twelve hours. It was like the writings that let him look into the soul of his grandfather, but now he was looking into the soul of God.

And the little notes inside the Bible, they were of great help. His grandfather must have spent his life studying this book. He noticed so many things that Paul was sure he never would have noticed.

Paul sat back and marveled for a moment. He thought about how his grandfather's manuscripts and cameras had had remained up in that old room of his for almost thirty years, collecting dust, because on the surface they appeared to be without value. At first glance, he'd thought the cameras were outdated and had almost thrown them away.

Wasn't that like his attitude towards religion? To him it seemed outdated. The Bible was just a stuffy old book filled with names no one could pronounce, but when he looked beyond the surface appearance, he discovered a treasure.

Paul's readings of the Bible made him feel as though he was starting to know God, just as his readings of his grandfather made him feel as if he knew him, but this new relationship soon turned into actual conversations in prayer. Paul surprised himself eventually by attending church. Like his grandfather, he went from one to another. Each of them seemed convinced that they did things just the way God wanted while the other churches were largely deluded. Oh there was hypocrisy, rivalry, gossip, and envy in almost all of them, but there was also the presence of God as they heard the scriptures and struggled to understand them more fully.

He shocked his friends when he decided to join one. It was far from perfect, but then again, so was he. There was something about belonging to a community where people encouraged one another to grow closer to God that seemed right. Sometimes he could feel God the most fully when he was with other believers.

His new church was far better than most at welcoming new people without judging them or forcing them to believe or behave exactly the same. They were not as quick as others to disown you when you walked a different path. Even Grandpa would have been welcomed here and accepted as he was. After saying his vows and receiving baptism, Paul saw coy smiles from the other members. He was part of the family now. He realized his newfound faith had changed everything in his life. He breathed a grateful silent prayer.

As he returned to his seat, the organist started a hymn, "Lord of the Dance."

Paul smiled. *Thanks Grandpa,* he thought

Paul knew in heaven his grandfather and grandmother were looking down at him and smiling.

Temporal Madness

The Rich Fool

Jim Edell pushed the roofing sealer over the huge black surface above his chicken coop. The sun was sweltering. He could see waves of heat rising from the tarry span before him. He paused for a moment to wipe his brow and gazed over the vast expanse of his farm. He looked at the two new barns, the sugarhouse, and the small lumber mill he'd erected last summer. It was going to take a lot of hard work to pay for it all, but in the end, it would be worth it. He started to think about all the projects he had to complete before the harvest season started and took a deep breath.

"Oh well," he said, "I can't make any money standing here doing nothing." And with that, Jim picked up a large bucket of sealer to pour on the next area.

"Mr. Edell?" called a voice from below him.

"That's me," he replied, as he put the bucket back down. He climbed down the ladder to meet a well-dressed man with a briefcase.

"I'm Jim Edell," he said, "and who might you be?"

"A pleasure to meet you, Mr. Edell," said the stranger. "I represent Mr. Arlan Feidler. I'm his attorney. Mr. Feidler asked me to serve you with these papers. You're to appear in court on August 13th concerning the civil suit described in these documents."

"Why, that no-good rattlesnake!" snapped Jim angrily. "He knows darn well I kept my part of the bargain. He sues everybody. He's a thief pure and simple. He just uses you high priced mouthpieces to make it all seem legal."

"It was a pleasure to meet you too, Sir," said the lawyer as he turned away to leave. "Mr. Feidler sends his regards, and we're both looking forward to meeting you in court on the 13th."

"He knows darn well that's my busiest time of the year. He's trying to ruin me. I've got enough things on my mind to take care of without all this nonsense to distract me."

Jim stopped shouting when it became obvious the lawyer wasn't even listening to what he was saying and then climbed back up the ladder, muttering things under his breath.

If there was one thing Jim hated, it was lawyers, especially those from the fancy Ivy League schools in the Northeast, who wore those fancy clothes and used all those fancy words to show how smart they were. The only thing he hated more was politicians. All they ever seemed to do was to sit around and come up with new regulations to make his work more confusing and less productive.

When Jim got back on the roof, his rage exploded. He wanted to punch his fist into a wall, but since there weren't any walls around he slammed his foot into the bucket of roofing sealer. This was a big mistake. He slipped on some of the wet sealer and started rolling down the side of the roof. He tried to grab for something to hold on to, but there was nothing but the slippery, black liquid, which stuck to his skin like fresh paint. Suddenly, he was falling and then everything was black.

The next thing Jim knew, a brilliant light was right in front of him. "Jim Edell," said a voice from within the light, "your time has come. You must leave this plane of existence."

"But I can't!" said Jim. "If I don't make some payments by Friday, I could lose my farm."

"Your farm should be the least of your worries right now," said the voice. "I don't think you understand the magnitude of the situation you are in. You are dying; you are leaving everything behind for good."

"But I've got responsibilities, I owe the IRS a lot of money....folks are coming to fix my tractor on Wednesday. I've got to get that hay in soon or I'll lose it... I've got to... Look! I can't die right now, I don't have time for it!"

"I'm afraid you have no choice in this matter," said the voice.

Slowly it all began to sink in. "Oh, Dear Lord," said Jim. "My wife, my kids, my Dad...I'll never see them again, will I?"

"Perhaps not," said the voice.

"Oh Lord, there's so much I wish I'd said to them. There's so many things I wish I'd done."

"You had plenty of time," said the voice. "Now you must leave them."

"But...but...can't I at least say good-bye to them?"

"In extreme cases, once in a great while, I let people say good-bye, but I really don't know if this quali—"

"Please?" said Jim.

"All right," said the voice, "but you'll only have a moment with each one."

Suddenly, Jim found himself standing in front of an old house. It was evening, and the crickets were chirping. He could hear the brook down the hill babbling. It brought back a myriad of memories of fishing with his dad. He still remembered that salamander that they'd found under a flat rock. He was afraid to touch it, but his dad had scooped it up so he could see it before he set it free. He remembered dozens of tall tales his father had told him while they sat on the banks together, catching nothing but perhaps a few rays of sun. When he was young he used to believe the stories and they set his imagination dancing merrily inside his head, but as he got older he learned to play along with the stories so that he and his dad both could pull a few over on his little sister.

Jim looked at the old house. He'd lost his mother years ago, but, in spite of his age, his father still kept the old place up pretty well.

Suddenly, the screen door squeaked and opened and an elderly man shuffled out on to the porch. "What's all the commotion out here?" the old man said. "What are you dogs barking about so crazy-like?"

Jim's father froze in his tracks as he looked at him. "Jim, is that you?" he asked.

"Yes," said Jim.

"Well what in tarnation are you glowing like that for? You been plantin' crops over by that nuclear power plant again?"

"Well, Dad, actually..."

"Wait a minute," said his Father. "You're a ghost, aren't you? You must have kicked the bucket."

"Well, yeah, but jeeze, I didn't know it would make me fall off the roof."

"It figures," said his father. "I knew it had to be something important. You never stop by here unless you want to borrow money or get me to co-sign a loan so you can buy some more equipment. What do you want this time? You want me to take over the farm for you?"

"Well, hey..." Jim thought about the idea for a moment...maybe it wasn't such a bad idea. He hated to think of all that work going to waste, but then he snapped back to reality when he realized it might be the last time he'd ever see his father again.

"No, Dad, I...I just wanted to tell you..." Jim felt a lump forming in his throat. He didn't know if he could say it. " I just wanted to tell you..."

Suddenly Jim was in darkness again with the bright light in front of him.

"Hey," said Jim, "I didn't get a chance to say what I wanted to say."

"I told you, you had only a moment," said the voice. "Don't let other things distract you. Say exactly what you want to say."

At once, Jim was in his own kitchen. His wife was at the sink washing dishes. He could hear the television from the family room in the back of the house. The kids were probably back there. Jim looked at his wife for a moment. She was beautiful. He hadn't stopped to look at her in a long time. He'd forgotten just how beautiful she was. She seemed to sense that she was being watched. She turned around and gasped when she saw him.

"Mary," said Jim, "I love you."

She smiled. "I love you too, Jim," she said, "but my name's Susan, remember?"

"Oh yeah, but someone's named Mary."

"She's, our daughter, remember?"

"Oh yeah," said Jim.

Susan embraced him and he held her as though he never wanted to let go. He remembered the first time he'd met her. He'd fallen in love with her almost at once, just like almost every other man who met her, and just like he was with almost everything else in his life, he was persistent. He wrote to her, took her out to the nicest places, and treated her like an absolute queen until, at last, she had agreed to spend her life with him.

"Do you remember that night when I asked you to marry me?" asked Jim.

"Yes," Susan whispered softly. "That special restaurant, that special music, that little walk we had in the moonlight. You made me feel like I was the most important woman on earth. I remember all the times we went out while we were still in high school. You used to want to be with me every moment, you used to want to hug me and kiss me more than you wanted to breathe. It even scared me sometimes. I was afraid that I wouldn't be able to stop you, until I finally learned the secret."

"What was that, darling?" asked Jim.

"I married you."

The words hit Jim hard. Susan stepped away from him.

"Once we got married, all you cared about was your farm. You were always building things or finding some other way to make more money and take up more of your time. You never had time for me and the kids. You don't even know me anymore. Sometimes you seem like a stranger right here in your own house."

"That's not true!" said Jim, "I..."

Suddenly a young boy ran into the room and bumped right into Jim.

"Young man," snapped Jim angrily, "who are you and what are you doing in my house?"

"I'm Billy, your son, remember?"

"Oh yeah, Gee, I'm sorry. Listen, Willy..."

"BILLY!"

"Oh yeah, Billy, listen, something terrible has happened. You see, I just died, but I came back so we could talk one last time and take care of some important things, but we only have a few seconds."

"OK, Dad," said Billy, "hey, if you're dead you won't be needing your tools anymore, can I play with them now?"

"Son, don't you realize...."

"Can I, Dad, please?"

"Well, sure Willy, but listen, I just wanted to tell you that I love you and I'll be watching out for you, and I hope you really strive to make wonderful things happen in your life."

"Don't worry, Dad, I'm going to be the best lawyer that Harvard ever put out!"

A little girl skipped into the room as Jim choked on the word, Lawyer. "And I'm going to run for Congress!" she said excitedly.

"Nooo!" screamed Jim. He was back in the darkness with the bright light standing in front of him.

"Wow," said Jim. "I guess I blew it, didn't I? I had a great father, a wonderful wife, and two wonderful children, and I never realized how important they were to me until it was too late."

"You left out one person," said the voice.

"Who?"

"Me."

"Well, who are you anyway?"

"I'm the one who created you. I'm the one who reached out to you thousands of times to try to show you the trap you were in. I was the one who could have been closest of all to you. and yet you always turned away from me."

"I'm sorry," said Jim, "But I guess we'll have a little time to get to know each other now, won't we?"

"I'm afraid not," said the voice. "It has been decreed that you will spend eternity with your greatest love. That was not me, nor was it your children, nor was it your wife. The greatest love in your life was yourself and your farm, so from now on you will spend all eternity at a huge farm all alone."

The word "alone" echoed over and over in Jim's head.

Then he heard other voices.

"He's about to come out of it," said one voice.

"How do you know?" asked another.

"Did you see the way he clicked his heels together and kept saying, 'There's no place like home.' over and over…that's a dead giveaway. Better go get his wife."

Jim's eyes fluttered open. "Where am I?" he asked.

"You're at Mercy Hospital," said a man in a white jacket.

"You fell off your barn roof and bumped your head pretty bad. We thought we were going to lose you for a while."

Susan ran into the room and embraced her husband.

"Oh, darling," said Jim, "I love you so much! I'm so sorry I married you!"

"What?" asked Susan.

"I mean, I'm sorry I stopped treating you like I used to before we were married. I want to sell the farm and just spend time with you and the kids…And with God."

"Wow, you really did bang your head, didn't you?"

"No, I'm serious," said Jim. "And…and another thing! Starting today, you are to forbid Billy from ever watching "Perry Mason" again. Is that clear?"

Luke 12: 13-21

Maximum Security

The huge, dark gray, concrete complex seemed threatening as Rita got out of her car and walked toward it. Two guards walked on either side of her. She noticed another on the roof. At the main gate, one of the guards pushed a button and then spoke into an intercom. After stating who they were and what their business was, a loud "click" signaled that the guard inside had tripped the electronic lock so that it could be opened.

The huge gate clanged shut behind them as they entered the courtyard. Rita felt claustrophobia already and she wasn't even inside the building yet. There were more locks and security checks as they entered and finally the small party walked down a long hallway decorated by video monitors and automatic doors. The final steel gateway had an elaborate security lock requiring one of the guards to place his palm on a sheet of glass to be read by a scanner.

The room Rita entered was pleasant, with soft chairs and a carpet, but the window, which covered most of the one wall, was made of thick, bulletproof glass reinforced with thick metal rods.

After a moment Charles, her husband, entered the room on the other side of the glass. "Honey," he said into his microphone, "how nice to see you."

"It's nice to see you, too" she answered. He knew something was wrong. He must have read her expression. The smile left his face.

"I can't remember the last time you came here to see me," Charles said, "what's the occasion?"

"Do I have to stand behind this sheet of glass to talk with you?" Rita asked.

"Oh, I'm sorry," said Charles. "It's been so long since I've let anyone back here I think I've forgotten how to open it."

Charles laughed as he searched behind an elaborate desk for the right switch. After a moment, the glass panel slid open.

"Come on in, have a seat," said Charles.

Rita started to sit, but Charles gasped as he saw what she was doing.

"No, no, no….not that chair, please!" he said quickly. "I'm sorry, that chair was made for Louis XIV, himself. It's not really for sitting... it's more for decoration."

Rita moved to another chair, but noticed that Charles grimaced again. "Can't I sit in this chair either?" she asked.

"Yyyyes, you can sit in the chair….it's just that…that Persian carpet you're walking on….an exclusive craftsman custom-made it for me…it's priceless…but I guess your feet are clean…it wasn't raining outside, was it?"

"No," said Rita as she stepped carefully to the chair and sat down.

Charles brushed off the large executive chair behind his desk before he sat down, as though he was afraid of getting a stain on his Italian tailored suit.

He took a deep breath and said, "Well." The single word conveyed a lengthy message. *I'm a busy man, I'm trying to be polite, but I wish you'd get to the point of why you are here so I can get back to my work.*

"You've remodeled again, haven't you?" Rita asked.

"Yes, I have, Dear. Now, what was it you wanted to talk with me about?"

"Oh, nothing really. It's just that I hardly ever get to see you anymore, and I thought maybe we could spend the afternoon together."

Charles let his face fall into his hands. "You told me you had to talk with me so I canceled a meeting with a client who purchases more than $10 million worth of merchandise every year after he'd flown out here to see me from the Middle East, and you just want to spend an afternoon together?"

Charles worked quickly to regain his composure. "Well," he said, "what would you like to do?"

"How about if we go for a ride in your Ferrari?"

"Honey, you know we can't do that. That car's my pride and joy. What if some kid threw a rock at it? What if I scratched it? Besides, I'd have to organize a motorcade and that would take just too much time. When you've got as much money as we have there's always someone who wants to take it. We've got to have protection."

"It's Jimmy's birthday today, you know," said Rita.

"Oh, is that what this is all about. Did someone forget—"

"Oh, no," Rita said, "that person you hired to take care of the little personal things in your life did his job just fine. He sent a nice card to Jimmy. I think he actually got your signature on it, this time, and then he drove him, his bodyguards, and those playmates he buys to the new video arcade you bought him."

Charles smiled, "A video arcade. That was a great idea. I'll have to give Fletcher a raise for that one."

"Jimmy doesn't know how to be a kid," said Rita angrily. "He can't go anywhere without a bunch of bodyguards. His friends are all afraid of him. He doesn't know what it's like to have a friend who likes him for what he is. They all like him for his swimming pool, his boat, his trampoline, his go-carts, or now his video arcade."

Suddenly, the phone rang.

"This had better be important," said Charles into the phone, "I told you not to disturb me.. Alright, yes, I understand. Yes, you were right, sell it now before it goes any lower. Call me back if...no, if anything else like this happens just make the decision yourself; you have my permission."

"Now," said Charles as he hung up the phone, "where were we?"

"Charles," said Rita, "there's something else."

Though she tried to fight it, tears began to fill her eyes.

The phone rang again.

"What now?" said Charles "He is? Didn't you tell him? OK...OK..."

"Rita, Honey," said Charles, "I'm sorry, but you know that guy from the Middle East I told you about earlier? He's outside right now and he's insisting on seeing me."

The first tear trickled down the side of Rita's face.

"Tell him I can't see him," said Charles into his phone.

Charles got up from behind his desk and knelt beside his wife, putting his arm around her shoulder. "What's wrong?" he asked.

"You love your job more than you love me," she said.

"That's nonsense," Charles replied. "I do this job *because* I love you. Haven't I bought you whatever you wanted? Don't I send you gifts? Don't I go out of my way to show you?"

"Oh, yes," said Rita, "you buy me jewelry, and cars, and all kinds of nice things, you even hire people to spend all day looking for things that I'll like."

"I have to honey, I just don't have the time to search for things myself."

"You know what my favorite gift from you was?"

"What?" Charles asked.

"That copper pendant that you bought me at that carnival."

"What??"

"You remember, back when we were in high school. You bought it in one of those machines where you could stamp your own message on a penny. Do you remember what you wrote?"

Charles blushed. "Yeah," he said, "That was silly...I even goofed one of the letters on it."

"That was the first time I knew that you loved me," said Rita. "It meant a lot to me."

Rita reached inside her blouse and pulled out a small copper pendant on a chain. "I still wear it."

Charles tried to speak, but he couldn't.

"Remember that summer when we were both camp counselors?"

"Remember that hayride and that haunted house at Mrs. Larson's place? Remember that old Volkswagen you used to drive? I liked that car best. We were always together when we drove that one."

"I was always embarrassed to pick you up in that," said Charles. "It was so old and beat-up. I thought you wouldn't want to be seen with me. I always swore someday I'd get you something nice. Something like you deserved. That's why I went into business with my father. We built this out of nothing, but it was all for you."

"Look what your success has done to you," said Rita. "How is this building different from a prison? You think you're locking other people out. I say you're locking yourself in. You've got chairs you can't sit in and rugs you can't walk on and a car that just sits in a huge security building because you're afraid to use it. We were better off with that Volkswagen. We never worried about scratching it because it probably would have improved its appearance. If we lost everything we had, it wouldn't have meant much back then because we didn't have much. We could sleep at night without worrying about '*things*.'"

Rita took an envelope out of her purse and handed it to Charles. "This is for you," she said, "It's from your mother."

Charles started to read the letter and turned pale. "This is a joke, isn't it?" he said, "You're just trying to teach me a lesson, right?"

"I'm afraid not," Rita replied. "Your mother inherited your father's entire share of the business. If she wants to give away all the buildings, equipment, and grounds to charity, she can."

"But we just took out loans. The business will fall apart. I'll have to sell everything I have to break even. She's senile. I'll talk to my lawyer. I'll..."

"She's perfectly sane." said Rita. "She said her husband died when he was 42. That's the year he started the business with you. Oh, he kept working till he was sixty, when he died, but your mother said she never knew him after that. She said she didn't want to see the same thing happen to her son and to me."

"How could she do this?" asked Charles.

"I asked her to," said Rita.

The words hit Charles hard. He was silent. For a moment, Rita feared he might strike her, but suddenly he wrapped his arms around her and whispered, "Thank you."

Charles and Rita walked out of the large concrete building arm in arm. Security guards started to walk beside them, but Charles told them that they could take the day off.

Charles took a deep breath and gazed at the garden he had never taken the time to look at.

"Where are we going?" asked Rita.

"I'm going to have to sell my Ferrari," he replied. "I thought maybe we could look for a Volkswagen."

Deleritus Locutio

Mad Talk

Jaws

The Gregory family said different words each night during dinner, but the script was always the same.

"A funny thing happened today at work, Hon," said Mr. Gregory, "Bob Anderson dropped one of those—"

"Billy!" shouted Mrs. Gregory, "How many times have I told you not to eat with your fingers? Now put that back and use a fork."

"I'm sorry, Dear. What were you saying?" she said to her husband.

"Uhh...oh, Bob Anderson...he dropped a live crayfish—"

"I thought you pronounced it 'crawfish'," said Mrs. Gregory.

"Whatever," said Mr. Gregory, "Anyway, Bob Anderson dropped a live crayfish or crawfish or whatever you call it into..."

"Billy!" shouted Mrs. Gregory again, "what did I just tell you? Honestly! I can't understand why you never listen to me."

Mr. Gregory waited until it was quiet again. "Well anyways," he said, "as I was saying, Bob Anderson dropped a live crayfish into..."

"Oh!" said Billy, through a mouthful of mashed potatoes, "guess what happened to me in school today?"

"Billy," said Mrs. Gregory, "how many times have I told you not to talk with food in your mouth? Now, swallow your food and try again."

Billy gulped loudly. "Today in school," he said, "the teacher told me and Jim she's gonna..."

"'Gonna?'" said Mrs. Gregory. "What kind of a word is 'gonna'? Have you ever seen a 'gonna' walking down the street? Are you sure you don't mean 'going to'?"

"Yes, Mother," groaned Billy, "Anyways, she said she's gonna get..."

"Wait a minute!" said Mr. Gregory, "I haven't finished MY story yet."

"I'm sorry, Billy," said Mrs. Gregory, "I guess you'll just have to wait until your father finally finishes his story. You know how he is sometimes."

Mr. Gregory took a deep breath. "Today, Bob Anderson dropped a live crayfish down the foreman's pants and he danced around like a..."

"Ha, ha, ha, ha!" Mrs. Gregory pointed out the window. "Look at those kittens out there playing with that paper sack," she said. "One hides inside and the other one waits to pounce on him when he comes out. I swear they're just like a couple of little kids."

Mrs. Gregory and Billy continued to stare out the window, laugh, point, and comment as Mr. Gregory went on with his story. "The foreman finally had to take his pants down to get it out," he said, "and by the time he got them back on, everyone..."

Mr. Gregory paused and looked at his family for a moment.

"As soon as he got his pants back on," he continued, "he went into his office and came out with a chainsaw. He killed Anderson and everybody else except for me. I managed to sneak out the loading dock, but he saw me running across the parking lot and shouted out the window that he'd hunt me down and kill me, my wife, my son, and even our dog!"

Mrs. Gregory continued to stare out the window. "That's nice, Dear," she said. "Oh, look at those kittens now. I swear they're just like a couple of kids."

ii

Mr. Gregory quickly finished his work and got ready to leave for home. This was it: the night of the big game. He couldn't wait to go home and watch it.

"Hi, Bill."

Mr. Gregory looked up to see Joe, one of his workmates.

"Have a few minutes to talk?" he asked.

"Well, I really do have to—"

"It's real important," said Joe.

"Well, maybe if it will just take a minute."

"It's about my wife," said Joe, "You know we've been having some trouble. She...she called me today on my cell phone and said she's moving out. She said I'm not—"

Mr. Gregory looked at his watch. The biggest game of the season and this had to happen? If he didn't start for home right now he'd miss the pregame show. He thought about taking the back road home. It was a little longer, but he could drive it faster and maybe shave off a couple minutes from his trip.

"...and she said I was no good at making money, I was no good in bed, I was boring, and I ought to just do the world a favor and kill myself," said Joe. "Do you think she had any cause to say that? ...Do you...Bill?

"Huh?" said Bill.

"I said, 'Do you agree with what she said?"

"Uh, well, of course I do, Joe."

Bill looked at his watch again. "Listen Joe, I've got something important going on at home. Can we talk about this later?"

Joe looked away. "Yeah, sure," he said.

Mr. Gregory made it home with only a few moments to spare. He tossed a pizza in the microwave and poured himself a tall cold one.

"Honey, I'm glad you're home," said Mrs. Gregory. "We need to talk."

"Whatever it is it will have to wait," he said. "I've been waiting all week for this game, and nothing is going to stop me from enjoying it."

"But-"

"No 'buts', Honey. I love you, but it will just have to wait."

Mr. Gregory became so engrossed in his game he didn't notice when his son came home from a friend's house. He took off his boots, threw his coat on the floor, and then ran to his father.

"Dad, Dad, guess what!" he shouted.

"SHHHHHH! Billy, can't you see I'm watching an important game?"

"But Dad, I-"

"Shhhh! Billy, I'll talk with you later, but for- OH, SHHH....! Billy, they just made a touchdown and you made me miss it. Now get out of here so I can watch the replay."

"I'm sorry, Dad, I-"

"Billy! I'll talk with you later, now just leave me alone."

After the game, Mr. Gregory sat in his easy chair and picked up the evening paper to catch up on the news. Billy timidly entered the room.

"Dad?" he said.

"Yes, son?"

"You said I could talk with you later."

"Yes, I did," said Mr. Gregory. He turned a page in the paper and continued to read.

"The teacher in school told me and Jim that she's gonna....Da'ad!"

"What?"

"You're not listening."

"Yes, I am. You said that your teacher told you and Jimmy something. I can hear you and still read the paper."

Billy scowled.

"Well?" said Mr. Gregory. "Go ahead."

Billy stomped his foot. "Da'ad!" he said.

"Oh, all right," said Mr. Gregory, putting his paper down roughly. "TALK! I'm listening."

Billy started to cry and left the room.

"Kids!" said Mr. Gregory. "I'll never understand them."

Epilogue

In the years that passed, Mrs. Gregory got tired of being ignored by her husband. Eventually she ran off with a mime artist from France. Around him, she could do all the talking.

Mr. Gregory didn't notice his wife was missing for three months, as he had never paid attention to her anyway. Eventually, he would die in a house fire. His son tried to warn him to get out, but unfortunately the Superbowl was on at the time.

Little Billy Gregory followed in his parents' footsteps. His ability to talk constantly without ever listening enabled him to get elected to Congress.

Speak No Evil

Al walked through the front door and grinned.

"Al, what have you got behind your back?" Sue asked.

"It's a secret, and I'm not going to tell you no matter what you do. You can torture me, you can put out my eyes, you can—"

"Al, come on, what is it? You can tell your little Suzy Quezy,"

Sue fluttered her eyelids and blew Al a kiss.

"Al, I'm being cute. You know you can't resist me when I'm being cute."

"Oh, all right, you win," said Al. "Here."

Al handed Sue a gift-wrapped box.

"Oh, Al," said Sue, "You shouldn't have!"

"All right, I can take it back." Al reached for the box.

Sue jerked the box away. "Don't even think about it," she said.

She tore open the box, looked inside, and then stopped, as though spellbound. "Oh, Al," she breathed, "where did you ever find it?"

Al beamed. "It wasn't easy," he said.

It hadn't been easy. Al looked through flea markets and household sales constantly, always hoping to find something like he had just found. Inside the box was a small statuette of Michael Jackson with its head attached to a spring so it wobbled.

"Oh, Al," said Sue almost in tears, "you're so good to me."

Sue threw her arms around Al and gave him a long hard hug. Then she took the statuette and brought it over to a large bookshelf covered with Michael Jackson memorabilia.

"I'm running out of room on my shelves," she said. "I guess we'll have to get a Michael Jackson *room* soon."

Sue placed the statuette on the shelf. *Why does he keep buying me this junk?* she wondered. *I mean yeah, when we were dating in high school I thought it was great, but I'm 38 years old, for crying out loud. I get so embarrassed when my friends come over and see this silly Jackson shrine. They must think I've never grown up.*

Al watched Sue. *Sheese,* he thought. *You would have thought she would have grown out of that silly thing she has for Michael Jackson by now. She's 38 years old for heaven's sake. I get so embarrassed when my friends come over and see that silly Michael Jackson shrine.*

ii

"For God so loved the world—"

Bill jerked to attention in his pew. He was thinking about the remodeling he was going to do in his study when Pastor Smith suddenly started yelling from the pulpit.

He surreptitiously glanced at his watch. Yep…it was 11:45. The preacher was working his way up to the conclusion of his sermon. He almost always shouted something right about this time; it was usually a familiar verse, like John 3:16.

"….that he gave his only son. That whosoever believeth in him should NOT perish but have…*everlasting life!*"

Bill waited. The preacher would say a couple of sentences softly and then he'd pound his fist on the pulpit. He always did that. Finally, he'd give a stirring altar call in a pleading voice. He'd tell everyone that this might be their last chance.

Boy, I'm getting sick of this, thought Bill. *He's been preaching to the same people for the last six years. Anyone who's going to come forward would have done so long ago. Why does he do it? Why does he preach the same old thing week after week? Doesn't he ever have questions like me? Doesn't he ever hunger for more advanced spiritual things? Doesn't he have the desire to tackle some major theological issues?*

Pastor Smith pounded his fist on the pulpit then closed with his usual pleading altar call.

As Bill walked out of the church, Pastor Smith shook hands with him. "Morning, Bill," he said.

"Morning," he replied, "Pastor Smith, you've charged me up for another week. I'm glad to know at least one person who's so consistent and rock solid with his beliefs. I enjoyed your message very much."

Pastor Smith looked at Bill's smiling face. *Why does he have to hear the same stuff week after week?* he asked himself. *You'd think he'd get bored after a while. Every sermon has to have the same old scriptural passages, a couple of shouts, a whack on the pulpit, and then I have to close with an altar call. Doesn't he ever wrestle with questions, like I do? Doesn't he ever hunger for more advanced spiritual things? Doesn't he ever have the desire to take on some major theological issues? Oh well, Bill and his friends are paying my salary, so I guess I have to preach on their level, but oh, how I'd love to make a few changes.*

iii

Klaus stared at the radio as the Fuehrer's voice pealed out of it. Col. Hamel seemed mesmerized. He was eating every word. Sgt. Wagner and Lt. Schmitt also listened with undivided attention.

What's wrong with these men? he thought. *Can't they tell he's a madman? He's got the whole world fighting against us, he preaches hatred and violence, He blames everything on the Jews just because they're Jews, and yet these idiots follow him just like sheep. They do whatever he tells them.*

Good Lord, he thought, *I'd like to just tear the swastikas off my shirt and stomp out of here in disgust, but if I did that—*

He wiped off the blood that had spattered on his face with his sleeve. It had started to dribble into his mouth and the thought if it made him sick. For a brief moment, he looked at the body on the floor. It was David. He looked so much like his own grandfather. He'd seen him perform in Berlin before the war. He could make anyone laugh, even here at the camp.

David was smarter than most of the guards. He could tell when they were about to get brutal and distract them with his humor. His timing was amazing. Most of the guards didn't even catch what he was doing. He always seemed to stay near the children expressly for that purpose. Klaus could not understand how David could act calm and even joke in the presence of violence. The other prisoners viewed him as a miracle worker. Even the guards couldn't help but like him.

David probably volunteered to voice the concerns of the other prisoners, fully aware of the danger. He tried to use that sense of humor again, but he knew it wouldn't work. He was scared.

Klaus rubbed his knuckles and shuddered slightly. It wasn't his fault. Col. Hamel had given the order. If he had refused, it might be his body on the floor now instead.

To the right of Klaus, Sgt. Wagner glanced at the body. *Why did it have to be the old man?* he asked himself. *I liked him. He tried to get along with us. I had to do what I had to do. The Colonel ordered us. I wish none of this had ever happened. Hitler's a madman, but why is it only I can see that?*

To the left of Klaus, Lt. Schmitt stared at the radio. *If I glance at him,* he thought, *they might suspect how I feel. The poor old fool was only trying to help his people. Hitler's a madman. Why am I the only one who can see it? I wish I had the courage to try to stop what happened, but if I had tried, Col. Hamel or the others would have shot me. There was nothing I could do.*

Col. Hamel stared at the radio. *Why can't those ignorant fools see that Hitler's a madman?* he thought. *Dear Lord, the way they tore into that old man...if I had tried to protect him they probably would have turned on me.*

"Sieg Heil! Sieg Heil!" shouted all four men.

Klaus kicked the old man as he walked out of the room.

"Jew Dog!" he snapped.   The rest followed his example.

Aesop vs. the KSU Faculty Discussion Group

The Birckhurst Memorial Lounge at Karlsburg State College was a lovely place: dark wood paneling, nice carpet, and a fireplace off to the side. There was even a little kitchenette in the back for fixing drinks and refreshments. This was the place for entertaining visiting dignitaries and potential donors. It was also the meeting site of the KSU Faculty Discussion Group. Each week at this time, a group of professors gathered to expand their already mammoth intellects through lively discussion and debate.

Dr. Glen Johnson sat in an easy chair near the fireplace. In his mid-thirties, he was the youngest man present. He was a clean-cut man with a narrow tie, a button down collar, and a tweed jacket. He glanced at his watch. Wouldn't you know, Marlin was late as usual and it was his week to present the topic.

"You suppose he lost his car keys in the refrigerator again?" asked Dr. Conrad.

Both men laughed. Many professors had a reputation of having their heads in the clouds, but Dr. Marlin set a new standard. He was the head of the Philosophy department and was often so lost in his lofty thoughts he seemed to lose contact with reality.

The sound of loud cursing caused both men to look to the other side of the room. It was Dr. Kline. He'd burnt his fingers while trying while to light his pipe again.

Dr. Selby, in the kitchenette, snickered as he poured a drink on the counter beside his glass. After a moment, when he went to pick up his glass and saw the wet counter, he checked the bottom of the glass for a leak.

Franklin Pickett, one of the art instructors on campus, stared into his glass of beer. He seemed fascinated by the unusual patterns formed by the bubbles. He was a heavyset man in his mid-forties with shoulder-length hair. He wore a sweater with no shirt underneath and a pair of paint-stained jeans.

At last, Dr. Marlin arrived. He shuffled through the door with a briefcase in one hand and a paper he was reading in the other. Unable to see exactly where he was going, Marlin bumped into a post, said, "Excuse me" very politely and then, realizing where he was, moved to the large table and sat down. His colleagues quickly joined him.

"This is Thursday, isn't it?" Marlin asked.

"Yes," said Dr. Johnson, "and to answer your next question, this is the Faculty Discussion Group."

"Oh, yes, yes, of course," said Marlin. "This was my week, wasn't it?"

"Yes," replied Johnson.

"Did I send you copies of our discussion topic?" Marlin asked.

Johnson sighed. "Yes, you did."

"Oh, good, good," said Marlin, "I was hoping I hadn't forgotten. Oh, and by the way, Glen, how's your wife doing? Is she out of the hospital yet?"

"She's doing fine," said Johnson with a slight smile, "and, yes, she's out of the hospital. She's been out for about six months now. You had dinner with us last week, remember?"

"Oh, yes, yes, of course, how silly of me," said Marlin. "Let's get on with our meeting."

Dr. Marlin sat back in his chair and began glancing through his papers. After a long pause, he looked up at Dr. Johnson with a puzzled look on his face.

"Well?" he said.

"Well what?" asked Johnson.

"Let's get on with the meeting."

"Dr. Marlin," said Johnson, "you are leading the discussion this week."

"Oh, yes, of course. Right you are," said Marlin. "I remember what it was we were going to talk about, too. I thought it might be interesting to look at some of the most famous fables and myths from ancient literature and see what interpretations we could come up with. You should all have copies of the three short examples I wanted us to examine this week."

"Our first story," Marlin continued, "is Aesop's famous fable of the tortoise and the hare. Does anyone care to give us your interpretation as to what exactly this story means?"

There was a long moment of silence before Dr. Conrad finally spoke. "Don't be silly Morris," said Conrad, "any fool can see what Aesop observed in this story."

"Tell us," said Marlin.

"Obviously," said Conrad, "Aesop had noted that aerobic respiration is more efficient than anaerobic respiration. Aesop had documented a simple biological fact. A rabbit can get quick bursts of speed and strength because of the high concentration of fast twitch muscle fibers in its large quadriceps, but the energy of this burst of speed comes at great cost, as it is all anaerobic. Within moments the rabbit becomes fatigued and must rest to restore his energy. The tortoise, on the other hand, has no need to rest, as he has a constant supply of aerobic energy."

"Ralph, I'm sorry, but you've missed the point entirely," said Dr. Johnson. "What Aesop was talking about here was economics. He was trying to point out that, while free enterprise may bring about great economic booms, a slower, government-controlled economy is more reliable and more efficient."

"You're close Glen," said Dr. Kline, "but I'm afraid you're being overly specific. Let us remember that, in the time of Aesop, no one was giving serious consideration to economic theories. I believe the rabbit in this story, a mammal, a higher life form than the amphibious tortoise, represented the aristocracy of Aesop's age. While they seemed to be fast and powerful, Aesop speculated that someday the masses would win the race and overpower their masters. This political evolution would be slow, but unstoppable, just like the tortoise. Not surprisingly, it took nearly 2,000 years for Aesop's prophecy to come to complete fulfillment in many modern-day regimes."

Dr. Pickett laughed. "You're all such brilliant fools," he said. "This fable is a work of art. You can't melt it down into refined philosophical concepts or logical syllogisms. He wouldn't have needed to write it this way if you could. Aesop used words as an artist uses a brush. He painted us a picture rich in feelings and sensuality. The arrogant hare, zipping along to the point of exhaustion, as the tortoise slowly but endlessly plods along. The shock and horror of the rabbit as he awakes; the victorious triumph of the noble tortoise. It's a masterpiece!"

Dr. Selby smiled smugly. "If you men went to a museum of modern art you'd probably marvel for hours at the place where someone accidentally vomited on the wall. Don't you realize that this 'masterpiece' you're reading so much into is a fraud? If Aesop even existed, he was a very minor creative artist of his day. Most of the stories attributed to him existed in the literature of India hundreds of years before he was born, and other stories attributed to him were written many years after his death. I've seen documented evidence of this, while at the same time we have only two extant accounts that attest to the fact that Aesop ever even existed."

"The documentation surrounding the story we are now discussing," Selby continued, "suggests that Aesop didn't even write it, but not only that, it also suggests that it was originally written as a children's story with no great point intended other than entertainment."

"Can I say something?"

Everyone turned to see who had asked the question.

It was Sally, the seven-year-old daughter of the cleaning lady assigned to this building on weekends. She often sat and listened to the debates, but always before had been quiet.

"Yes," Marlin replied. "We'd like to hear your thoughts."

"My father is a carpenter," said Sally, "and he always says that when your only tool is a hammer, you tend to see all your problems as nails. Dr. Conrad, you see a story about muscle fibers because you teach about bodies and stuff. Dr. Kline, you see government things because that's what you teach. Dr. Pickett, you see an artistic masterpiece because you're an artist."

"If you ask me," Sally said, "I think the main message in that story is just that you do more by sticking with things than through short bursts of effort. In other words, slow and steady wins the race. Maybe I'm just stupid, but that's the way it looks to me."

"Thank you for sharing that," said Pickett.

"You're very insightful for your age," said Marlin.

"I think you'll be a professor someday," said Selby.

Sally's mother had overheard the exchange from another room and arrived looking sheepish. She took her daughter by the hand, apologized, and left quickly.

The professors smiled at each other, each amused by the ignorance of the uneducated.

"Well, let's move right along," said Marlin. "For our next story, I chose the Biblical story of creation, as found in the book of Genesis. Who would like to be the first to say what they think it means?"

"Don't be silly," said Dr. Selby. "Why should we waste our time discussing something so obvious? Any fool can see what that story means."

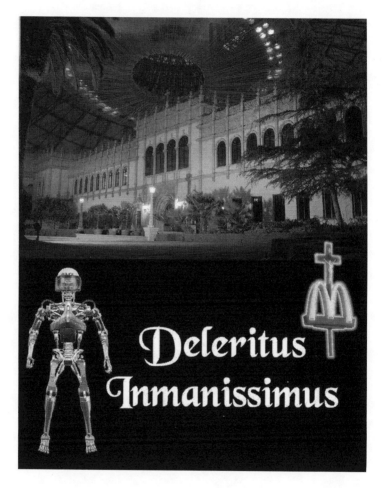

Deleritus
Inmanissimus

Extreme Madness

How John Messerschmidt Destroyed the World in his Sophomore Year

John Messershmidt sipped his beer slowly, unaware that his behavior this evening would result in the destruction of his entire planet. He was a sophomore at Miskatonic University near Arkham, a science major on a special scholarship from the physics department. Before he had even graduated from high school, his electronic wizardry had received international attention. His unhappy home life had inspired him to escape to his laboratory and take his mind off his problems by overloading it with complex theory and electronic design.

His friend, Harry, also from the physics department, had insisted that he come with him to the local watering hole to meet some women, and he had not taken "no" for an answer. John knew that there would be no women interested in him, but at least the beer would deaden his pain.

John looked at the men and women on the dance floor. They seemed so happy. Of course, *they* had someone to be with. Most of them had someone to love and cherish them. He knew he never would. He was a loser. No woman would ever want him.

John took several gulps of his drink and silently cursed his fate. It didn't seem fair that some people had all the luck while he had nothing but pain.

"Hi John!"

The voice was sweet and cheerful. John turned to see Mary Crawford, that pretty assistant from the biology lab. He'd spoken with her on several occasions and found her personality delightful.

"Oh, hi," John said.

"How nice to see you outside that dark laboratory of yours," she said. "I've never seen you before in your *civilian* clothes. You look very nice."

"Thanks," said John, blushing slightly, "you look very nice yourself."

John felt his heart race as Mary walked away. She sounded like she was interested in him. *No!* said a resounding voice inside his head. *Don't kid yourself. She was just being polite. She talks to everybody like that. What would a gorgeous babe like that see in a geek like you?*

Across the room, Mary tried to calm her pounding heart. He was here! John Messershmidt! That genius from the physics department whom she'd been dreaming of for months. It seemed too good to be true, but he actually seemed to be interested in her. Mary started hoping and praying that he would ask her to dance.

John watched Mary from across the room. She was *so* beautiful. He fantasized about how wonderful it would be to dance with her. *Stop it,* said the voice in his head. *You're just building yourself up for a big letdown.*

As the next hour passed, John became more depressed as he thought how cruel the world was. Beautiful women like Mary were put right in front of him, but he couldn't have them.

Mary grew restless. What could she do to show him her interest? She summoned her courage and walked over to the table where John and Harry were sitting.

"Hi," she said. "What are you boys up to?"

John tried to talk, but no words would come out. His throat felt paralyzed.

"We were just discussing John's latest project," said Harry.

"Oh?" said Mary, "What is it?"

"John has discovered a new form of radiation that travels faster than the speed of light. Furthermore, he devised a means of sending and receiving messages with this radiation just like you can do with radio waves. He's been using this device to send messages to the densest star clusters in our galaxy. He believes that he may be able to communicate with extraterrestrial life-forms."

"How exciting!" said Mary.

A new song started to play for the people dancing. "Oh!" said Mary, "That's my favorite song. I *love* to dance to it."

Don't even think it! said the voice in John's head. *If you ask her to dance, she'll laugh and you'll die right here, right now.*

"Gee," said Mary, "I sure wish I had someone to dance with."

There was a long uncomfortable silence, after which Mary looked hurt.

Harry cleared his throat. He looked at John and tried to gesture for him to move without looking too obvious.

"Um.... gee, Mary," Harry said at last, "anyone would be a fool not to take a sharp chick like you up on an offer like that." He looked at John, who just stared at his glass of beer.

"I'd like to dance with you," said Harry after an awkward pause.

Mary hesitated, but perhaps this would break the tension and encourage John to ask her to dance later.

"All right," said Mary, and she headed out to the floor with Harry.

John gulped down the rest of his beer and glared at the two as they danced. She liked Harry. He'd always known it. How could such things happen to him? It was bad enough that she wasn't interested in him, but she had to go after his friend right in front of him; she had to rub his nose in it. She'd probably sit right there at the table and cuddle up with Harry, right in front of him, for the rest of the evening. The more he thought about it the more hurt and angry he became.

After the song, Mary and Harry returned to the table. They tried to talk with John, but they could get little more than a grunt or two out of him. Mary worked to build up her nerve. Finally, when another song started, she asked John if he wanted to dance.

John rose to his feet angrily. "Why don't you leave me alone you stupid wench!" he shouted. With that, he slammed his chair under the table, spilling everyone's drinks, and stormed out of the building.

"She knows how I feel about her," John muttered, "She thinks she has to show sympathy. I don't need her sympathy! I don't need anyone."

"Women!" he shouted as he reached the sidewalk outside.

"Men!" said Mary as she wiped the spilled beer from her dress.

Harry ran into the parking lot ran after John. "What's wrong with you, man?" he said.

"Why don't you mind your own business!"

"It is my business. You're my friend. You just made a fool of yourself in there and I don't think you understand what—"

Suddenly John shot a fist into his friend's face.

This was a mistake. Harry stood 6'4" and weighed 210 pounds. Instinctively, he swung back and knocked John to the pavement.

"John, John! I'm sorry!" he said, but it was too late. John could no longer hear anything but his own anger raging inside him. He ran to his car, revved the engine, and then spun out of the parking lot, kicking up gravel and squealing the tires against the pavement.

Back at the university, strange things were happening. All the lights went out and nothing electrical worked. It seemed like a power failure, but even battery-powered radios shut off. Strange, arching rays of electricity began to appear all around the science building. By the time John arrived, there was a hurricane-like wind and a strobe-like series of brilliant flashes of light. People began to scream as a massive vehicle as large as the entire university appeared in the sky with a deafening roar.

John, however, remained oblivious to all this. He stormed up the steps to his third floor lab completely consumed by his rage. "Stupid women...." he muttered.... "Who needs 'em anyway. I'll go back to my lab. I'll show them. I'll—"

When John opened the door to his lab, he was surprised to see an alien that looked very much like a walking aardvark with an octopus for a head.

"Greetings, John Messershmidt," said the alien through some sort of communication device. Its voice was computer-like, but understandable. "We have answered your call. We have come to show you a cure for cancer, a way to ensure world peace, a way to—"

John kicked the alien in the midsection. "Don't start with me!" he shouted, "I've had a rough day!"

The alien ambassador was seriously injured by the attack. Those monitoring his vital signs on the mother ship beamed him back up immediately. When the aliens learned what happened they destroyed the entire planet with an antimatter bomb.

Negative thoughts can indeed lead to rather serious repercussions at times.

ALERT LA318

In the not so distant future...

Crimes of violence had become so commonplace in Los Angeles that people rarely ventured out in the open except in large groups. Pushers sold drugs openly on busy street corners, and local police officers were powerless to stop them. These were desperate times requiring desperate actions. After much debate, the city council decided to take drastic and controversial action.

The first Automatic Law Enforcement Robotic Troopers, or *ALERTs* as they were called, entered the city less than a month later. Cold and mechanical, they were devoted only to one thing: the total elimination of all forms of crime. They never tired. They could not be bribed. It did no good to argue with them. When they placed you under arrest, you did as they said or they would shoot you with machinelike precision. They didn't coddle criminals. Human emotions did not bridle them. They obeyed their directives precisely. Within the first week of their employment, they made more than 1,000 arrests. In the process, 514 suspects were killed and 94 wounded, with only 127 cases of notable collateral damage. Already the city was becoming a safer place to live.

Berlin Heights was an exclusive residential area in greater Los Angeles. When Anna Frederick, the wife of a well-known plastic surgeon, saw a couple of young hoods smoking dope near her front gate, she immediately called the police. ALERT LA318 was near the area and responded.

Chuck Reynolds and Bob Martin, dressed in suits and ties, their hair neatly arranged, approached the gate of the Frederick residence. They were home on spring break and were looking forward to going on a double date with Dr. Frederick's two daughters. Two young men running at top speed whizzed past them.

"Jeeze!" said Chuck, "Those guys practically ran us over."

Bob bent down and picked up a small smoking object. "Look at this," he said, "They must have really been in a hurry. They left a couple of reefers behind and they'd hardly even started smoking them. I wonder what spooked them?"

As if to answer his question, they heard loud, metallic thumps on the pavement around the corner. ALERT LA318 stepped into view. It looked like a huge man constructed of gleaming steel and blinking lights. It stopped, pointed a finger at Bob and said with a mechanical voice, "Young man you are under arrest for violation of State Code 501, section 2, paragraph three: possession of a controlled substance."

Bob looked at the marijuana in his hand and suddenly realized what had happened. "Hey, wait," he said. "It's not what it looks like. These two guys just dropped this and I just..."

"You have the right to remain silent," said the robot, "Anything you say can and will be..."

"Wait! Listen!" said Bob. "I didn't do anything and the guys who did are getting away!"

"You have the right to be represented by an attorney..." the robot continued.

"Look, I know my rights, would you just shut up and listen for a second!"

"He's right," said Chuck, "he didn't do anything. I saw the whole thing."

"I am now placing you under arrest for resisting arrest as well as for your previous offense," the robot droned. "I am charging your friend with aiding and abetting a criminal and obstructing justice. I would advise you both to walk quietly to my police car before I am forced to take stern action."

Mrs. Frederick came running from her house. "No, no," she shouted. "You've got the wrong boys! I'm the one who called you."

"I received my orders on my wireless digital transponder, Ma'am. I captured these suspects in the act of committing serious crimes. I would advise you to return home at once to avoid possible danger."

"Listen, you idiot. These boys have done nothing wrong."

"I have video footage now of the suspect holding a controlled substance in his hand. I have no choice but to arrest him."

"Those other kids must have dropped it and he must have just picked it up!"

"I am programmed to arrest this suspect."

"You're not listening!" Mrs. Frederick shouted. She pounded on his chest as she tried to explain things again.

"Madam," said the robot, "You are vandalizing valuable public property. I must place you under arrest. Please step quietly to my car."

"Would you freaking listen for a minute?" she said as she shoved the robot.

"I must warn you that I am programmed to protect myself. I am authorized to use deadly force when I am physically attacked. I must ask—"

Mrs. Fredrick's blind rage prevented her from hearing the warning. She continued to yell and punctuated her words by pushing the robot again. Suddenly, the robot drew his pistol and shot her in the chest. The force of the blast sent her flying backwards. The 50 caliber soft-tip magnum bullet did considerable damage."

"You monster, you killed her!" shouted Chuck. He jumped at the robot.

"BLAM" the pistol fired once more, hitting its target with deadly precision.

Bob couldn't take any more. He fainted. As he fell, his head struck the car behind him, leaving a bloody gash.

Alerted by the shots, Mayor Valdez, who lived across the street, ran to see what had happened. He looked at the three bodies on the sidewalk and turned pale. "Dear Lord!" he exclaimed. "What have you done?"

"In the process of arresting two criminal suspects, I was physically attacked and responded with deadly force, as I have been authorized."

"But these are good kids!" said the mayor, "and Mrs. Frederick, she's never done anything wrong in her life!"

"Two more senseless drug related deaths," droned the robot.

The mayor checked Bob's body. "Thank God," he said. "He's still alive, but he's bleeding pretty bad. We've got to call an ambulance."

The mayor checked his pocket for his cell phone, but he'd left it at home.

Panic blurred the mayor's thinking as he impulsively ran across the street to his house. He cursed when he discovered he had locked himself out.

Without thinking, he grabbed a rock and smashed a pane of glass beside the door so he could reach in and unlock it. The clanging sound of his alarm and the booming voice of the robot behind him made him realize at once that he had made a horrible mistake.

Valdez obeyed the order to freeze and the robot raced across the street to recite his rights.

"That boy across the street is bleeding," said Valdez. "Can't you radio for help?"

"You have the right to an attorney—"

"I know my rights, damn it. Just call a freaking ambulance."

"I am programmed to subdue dangerous felons before contacting support services. If you will lie face down while I handcuff you—"

Suddenly Valdez saw a car pull over and stop in front of the Frederick house. The girl in the car was a friend of the Frederick girls. She had two male friends with her. They got out and reacted with horror at the carnage they saw. The door of the house opened and Jamie and Andrea Frederick stepped out. They ran to the bodies, screaming.

"This is MY house," said Valdez. "The only thing I did wrong was to approve you monsters for use in our city. I am the mayor of Los Angeles. I represent all the people in this city. I order you to radio for an ambulance, drop your weapon, and wait in your car until I've talked with the police commissioner."

"I am not authorized to do anything other than what I have been programmed to do," said the robot. "You have ten seconds to lie face down and place your hands behind your back."

Valdez could hear the angry shouts across the street. The young men were looking at him with his hands up and the robot pointing a gun. They were shouting at the robot.

"Ten... nine... eight—" said the robot.

The Frederick girls and their friends started to cross the street. Valdez shouted for them to stay away, but they couldn't hear over their own angry shouting.

The boys would probably attack, it would be a massacre.

"...Three...Two..."

Valdez madly slammed into the robot. It was like hitting a steel wall. The bullet that entered his chest knocked him back into the glass panels beside his door. The glass shattered.

"I.....I am the mayor... I represent all the people in the city of...Los Angeles..." he choked, as his blood spilled on the ground.

ALERT LA318 turned, and his amplified voice echoed through the neighborhood. "Attention, people of Los Angeles, you are all under arrest for aiding and abetting a known criminal. I would advise you to walk quietly to my police car or I will commence firing."

McChurch

The Johnson family cruised down Interstate 93 silently. "I just don't feel right about this," said Mrs. Johnson. "I still think we should have gone to church before we left."

"But, Hon," said her husband, "We wouldn't have gotten home until 11:30, and then we would have had to get the kids ready and changed our clothes. By the time we left for the camp, half the day would be shot."

Mrs. Johnson opened her mouth to speak, but then turned to gaze out the window. Tacit approval through silence was better than open agreement. If only there was some way to do her duty to God and still enjoy Sunday.

Suddenly, off in the distance, she saw the familiar golden cross and arches, the symbol of a McChurch!

"Honey! Look!" she said.

"Well, I'll be!" said Mr. Johnson. "You kids want to stop at a McChurch?"

In the backseat, Jody and Tommy Johnson sprang to life. "Yes, yes!" they said.

"I want a Happy Feast!" said Jody

"Me, too!" said Tommy.

In a moment, they had pulled off the interstate and pulled up to a small wooden model of a church on top of a pedestal.

"Good morning," said a friendly voice from the speaker, "and welcome to McChurch. May I take your order please?"

"Um, yes," said Mr. Johnson. "We'll have communion for four people."

"Catholic or Protestant?" asked the voice.

"Protestant."

"What music would you like to go with that?"

Mr. Johnson thought for a moment. "What do you have?"

"We have, 'Contemporary Christian Favorites with Steven Curtis Chapman,' 'Bach's Sacred Organ works with Virgil Fox,' 'Metal for the Master with the Sons of Thunder,' or 'Hollerin' for Jesus with the Footstompin' Pentecostal Church of Spivey's Corners, Kentucky.'"

Tommy wanted the last one, but Mom and Dad overruled and got the organ music instead.

"What have you got for sermons?" asked Mr. Johnson.

"We have: 'You can Be a Selfish Pig for Jesus' by Jimmy Jacobs, 'Jesus is Coming Back and He's Pretty Ticked Off' by Rev. Larry Wright,' 'Satan is Kind of like the Democrats" by Dr. James Patterson,' 'Words like *Sin* are a little Extreme' by the Rev. Dr. Pendleson Love, and 'The Power of Possibility Thinking: Part 410' by Robert Schuller.'"

"We'll take the Schuller one, I guess," said Mr. Johnson.

"Thank you. Will that be all, Sir?"

"Yes."

"Daddy! What about our Happy-"

"Oh, yeah, almost forgot. We'd like two Happy Feasts for our kids."

"We're having a special on conversions today, Sir. Is your whole family saved?"

"Daddy, Daddy!" said Tommy excitedly. "I haven't been saved yet."

"But, you're too young."

"I am not. I'm six years old."

"Well, I don't know…"

"Come on, Dad. You let Jody get saved the last time we came here."

"Well, that was different."

"Please, Dad? I promise, I'll do my homework every day, I won't talk back, I'll even clean my room."

Mr. Johnson smiled. "I guess my six-year-old boy would like to get saved today," he said into the speaker.

"Your order comes to $19.95. But, today, if sign up to tithe regularly, we'll provide a free McFuneral when you die."

"No thanks," said Mr. Johnson.

"Thank you, Sir. Rev. Smith has already said the prayer of consecration over your communion elements. If you'll pull around to the side window, we'll take care of your order."

At the drive through window, Mr. Johnson took the items that were offered to him while Rev. Smith, a kind looking man with a well trimmed gray beard, stepped over to Tommy's window and motioned for him to roll it down.

"Do you sincerely want to accept Jesus Christ as your personal savior, young man?"

Tommy nodded silently.

Rev. Smith then recited a sinner's prayer and asked Tommy to repeat it.

As soon as Tommy was through, all the workers came running out of the McChurch. Many had tears streaming from their eyes. They all kissed Tommy on the forehead and welcomed him into the family of God, but before you could blink an eye, they were running back into the McChurch to get ready for their next order.

As they pulled back on to the highway, Mrs. Johnson reached inside the paper bag and pulled out a CD and slid it into the CD player. As the sounds of an organ played softly in the background, she pulled out a cardboard box. Inside was a piece of warm bread fresh from the oven. She broke it into four pieces and handed them to the other members of the family.

"The body of Christ," she said solemnly.

Next, she removed four small paper cups with covers and straws. She handed the grape juice to each of them.

"The blood of our Lord," she said.

When her children remained silent through this part, it impressed Mrs. Johnson, and she rewarded them by handing them their Happy Feasts. Both children opened their church-shaped boxes and removed a coloring book of McJesus stories, some crayons, some Testo-mints, and a Biblical action figure.

It thrilled Tommy to see that he had finally gotten the John the Baptist doll with the removable head.

Mrs. Johnson looked in the bottom of the bag and found the expected McBingo card. The winner would get a free luxury vacation to the Holy Land. With the edge of a coin she scratched off all the little silver squares, but, alas, no McBingo.

"One thing I'll say for these McChurches," said Mr. Johnson. "They're quick, inexpensive, and you don't even have to change your clothes to go to them."

Tommy was still on cloud nine following his conversion. "Do you think they'll have to change their sign to say '2 Billion and **1** Saved'?" he asked.

Everyone laughed.

Fairy Tales

Prophecy of Light and Dark

Once upon a time, a prince was born in the land of the Benthians. On the day of his birth, the royal family and all the nobles celebrated. The celebration had scarcely begun when a mysterious old man entered the throne room. All grew silent when they saw him. It was the oracle, who was always correct in his prophecies of the future.

"This child," he said, "has the ability to bring an end to the great war that has plagued your kingdom for three generations. He will be blessed with powers far beyond those of other great warriors. All who do battle with him will run in fear or fall before him, but he cannot succeed alone. He must find his true love, with hair the color of the sun, the fairest maiden in the world. Together they shall bring a generation of peace and love."

The people murmured at the hopeful news, until the oracle continued.

"His shall find his true love in the heart of the land of Chaiteil."

At the mention of Chaiteil several people gasped. Chaiteil was the land of their hated enemy. The people of this land were violent and practiced the darkest sorcery. None who entered the land returned alive.

The oracle continued. "The prince will face a great test of his courage and wisdom. If he passes the test, all will come to pass, as I have said. If he fails, the land will remain in darkness and war for three more generations."

Young Prince Galad indeed proved to be supernaturally gifted. At will, he could transform himself into a creature ten feet tall with claws of steel and the strength of a dozen men. Just the sight of him in this form was enough to send others running in terror, but anyone foolish enough to face him fell quickly before him.

The prince proved himself in combat again and again, easily defeating the evil invaders from the land of Chaiteil, but when he came of age, he knew he would have to face his destiny. His advisers warned him that, when he entered Chaiteil, he would no longer face mere mortals. His foes would attack with the darkest sorcery. His battles would be more fearful and dangerous than anything he had ever faced.

Galad did not hesitate. He set out for the land .alone.

As expected, the prince faced many terrible adversaries. The struggle was difficult, and many times, he felt he might be defeated, yet he always prevailed in the end. In time, the land became so threatening that he changed into his fighting form so that he would always be ready for attack.

When he reached the very heart of the land, he heard a deep snarl and turned to see a creature with steel claws longer and sharper than his own. He had barely survived his previous battles, but this was worse than anything he had faced.

The battle started at once. This creature had poison on its claws that stung and weakened Galad. Relentlessly, he struck as he tried to defend himself from the creature's onslaught, but his strongest blows seemed only to enrage it more.

At last, the two fell back. Galad noticed that he was bleeding severely and was growing weak, but he gained courage when he saw that he had severely wounded the monster as well.

Again, they engaged in combat. Both fought more fiercely than before, and when they fell back, each was wounded far more.

Galad realized that the next bout would surely kill one of them. He was about to step forward again, ready to risk his life to do his duty, when he remembered the words of the oracle. To succeed, he would need to have courage and wisdom. The oracle had said nothing about brute force or violence.

Galad looked at the horrifying appearance of his foe and realized that, in his fighting form, he probably looked horrifying as well. The monster he faced snarled and roared. Galad remembered that, when he was in his fighting form, those were the only sounds he could make also.

He decided to take the ultimate risk. He would return to human form so that he could talk. This would leave him vulnerable to the monster. The monster could kill him easily. In spite of the monster's beastlike appearance, it did appear to be intelligent.

Galad returned to his human form.

"If we continue this fight," he said, "one of us will die. I only want one thing. Give me my true love, the maiden with hair the color of the sun and I will leave this land."

The monster snarled and roared, but did not strike.

"It has been prophesized that, if I join with my true love, peace and love will fill our lands and the curse will be lifted," the Prince said.

The monster grew silent.

Trusting his own heart and ignoring everything he had learned about combat, Galad stepped toward the monster. He approached until the monster could easily kill him. The monster did strike, but not with full strength. Galad ignored the pain and stepped even closer. Finally, he embraced the creature. As he did, the creature started to change. It grew smaller. The fangs and claws disappeared. Suddenly in his arms was the most beautiful maiden in the world....with hair the color of the sun.

She trembled in fear. "But, you are from the land of Benthia!" she said through tears. "You people are violent and you practice the darkest sorcery."

"No," said Galad, "that is what we say about your land."

Both of them laughed, and it was the beginning of mirth and joy, which spread throughout two great kingdoms and led to a generation of peace.

The Keys of Truth

Once upon a time, there was a kingdom in which all the people wore shackles on their wrists and ankles. The people could not work very well with their arms shackled, but the king and the priests, who wore no chains on their hands, could do remarkable things. No one, not even the king or the priests, could run, however, because of the shackles on their legs.

The king and the priests alone had the power to release arm shackles, so all the people looked at them with awe. Now and then when someone served the king or the priests exceptionally well, they would say that he was worthy to have his chains removed. When his hands were free, the priests invited him to join them. This happened quite rarely.

Not far outside the kingdom was a forest the people were forbidden to enter. The king and the priests warned them that there was great danger there and they should never enter it. This was an open invitation for a young man named Christopher, because he was rebellious and disrespectful by his nature.

Although the king had never heard of Christopher, some of the priests knew of him. They did not look at him with favor because he didn't respect them or their traditions. He often got into trouble.

Christopher wondered why the forest was forbidden. It could be there were dragons there, or it could be there was treasure that the king and the priests didn't want anyone to find. Being disrespectful and rebellious by nature, Christopher suspected the latter.

Much to his disappointment, when Christopher entered the forest, he found neither dragons nor treasure. He was just about to leave when he noticed a gleam in the shadows. Following it, he found a glowing key. Inscribed on the key were the words, "The Second Key of Truth."

Christopher noticed at once that the key seemed exactly the right size to fit into the lock on his ankle shackles. He placed the key into the lock and, in a moment, was free. This stunned Christopher. His astonishment grew as he walked and saw how effortless walking now was. Then he started running. At first, it was difficult because he had never before tried this. He stumbled many times, but then he ran faster and faster. It felt wonderful!

When Christopher returned to his village, he shuffled along slowly so no one would notice, but late that night he gathered many of his young, rebellious friends and asked them if they noticed anything different about him. At first no one did, but then Christopher ran, danced and leaped in the air. He kicked the piece of hay that one of his friends was chewing right out of his mouth. His friend's jaw dropped. Some of his companions gasped; others covered their eyes with their hands.

"Your leg shackles are gone!" shouted one. "How did you do that?"

Christopher explained to them about the Second Key of Truth.

"Can you free us also?" his friends asked excitedly.

"Of course," said Christopher, and he did.

At first, they too stumbled, but soon all could run, and they laughed and celebrated.

"We must tell everyone!" exclaimed one friend.

"No!" warned Christopher, "If there is a Second Key of Truth, there must be a First Key. The king and the priests must have it. That is how they free their hands.

"Why haven't they shared it with us?" asked one friend.

"Don't you see?" said Christopher. "As long as they alone have the key they can be better than us. They can be kings and priests and live in castles and mansions. Everyone else can envy them. If they learn of this key they will want to hide it also."

"What can we do?" asked another.

"We must release people secretly," said Christopher, "and try not to draw the suspicion of the king or the priests. We must also find the first key."

"But how?"

"Use your head," said Christopher, "Where do you *think* they would hide it?"

When none of them could answer, Christopher reminded them that he had found his key in the *forbidden* forest.

"What else have they forbidden us access to?" asked Christopher.

"The Forbidden Book!" all his friends said together.

"But the Forbidden Book is deep inside the temple and guarded by hundreds of soldiers."

"Yes," said Christopher, "but none of them can run."

Late that night, Christopher and his followers crept up to the temple. They watched the guards shuffling along slowly. The guards were not very alert because the people in the kingdom moved so slowly they always had plenty of time to stop them, but not this night. When one of the guards turned his back, as quick as a flash Christopher and three of his friends raced into the temple. The guard thought he heard something and turned around slowly, but by that time, they were gone. He figured it was just his imagination since nothing could move that fast.

Inside the temple, Christopher and his friends made their way to the main sanctuary and there, in the darkness, they found the Forbidden Book. The gleam dazzled them when they opened the book. They took the key and freed themselves from their arm shackles.   Immediately they ran out of the temple.

There was great celebrating that night. Christopher and his friends clapped their hands and danced, feeling more free then they ever had before. The next day, they began to free people secretly. They warned everyone to be discreet about their new freedom, but, almost at once, one foolish person ran through his village dancing and singing with glee. He had trouble with his new freedom. He stumbled and hit his head on a rock. He was dead.

People watched the man and screamed. No one had seen a man without chains on his legs. They thought it was sorcery. A panic went through the kingdom. The king ordered all his soldiers to find out who was responsible for this outrage. They hunted Christopher and his followers for weeks, but they couldn't catch them because they were too fast.

At last, the king called a great assembly. Everyone in the kingdom was there.

"All of us must capture this outlaw, Christopher," he said. "He has violated our temple. He threatens to destroy our way of life."

Suddenly, from the back of the crowd, a defiant voice shouted. "Why don't you tell them the real truth!" he said.

"Who dares!" shouted the king.

Christopher boldly stepped out of the crowd.

"I dare," he said. "I have not violated the temple. You have."

"How dare you!" shouted the king. "We hold the only key of truth.   You deceive the people by saying there is another."

As guards rushed to arrest Christopher, he easily outmaneuvered them and leaped up onto the platform beside the king.

The people gasped in shock when they saw Christopher leap. It was impossible.

When he kicked the crown off the King's head, several screamed.

A great murmur came from the crowd. Some were in awe of Christopher, but some hated him for disgracing their king.

"Not only do I have the new key," shouted Christopher, "but I have the old key as well. My hands are as free as yours are. You have been keeping these keys to yourself so you and the priests could rule all others."

"The people can't handle the keys!" shouted a priest. "They will stumble and fall if they try to be like us. A man was killed because you set him free."

"At first they will stumble," said Christopher, "but if they are careful, soon they will run and leap like me. It will save lives when people can run from danger."

"If everyone is free, who will do the work?" demanded the king. "Everyone will be like a king."

"We will all share the work," said Christopher. "Even you and the priests. Why should you alone be privileged?"

Christopher's words excited many, but frightened and angered many others. They began to argue, and then fights broke out in the crowd.

"Listen to me!" shouted the king. "For hundreds of years we have lived in peace and harmony. Now this young upstart has brought nothing but trouble. Look how everyone is fighting and arguing."

The people had always followed the king. Christopher was new. The changes he suggested were frightening.

Suddenly, everyone started shouting. The chaos was frightening to a kingdom unacquainted with controversy. The soldiers and people were so used to following the king that they followed his orders without thinking. The sea of people surrounding Christopher and his friends soon overwhelmed them.

The king and the priests took both keys and locked them in their temple. They tried to put new shackles on Christopher, but each time they tried they would simply fall off his wrists or ankles.

"When the keys of truth free you," said Christopher, "you can never be confined again."

Christopher's public execution was clear proof to most that the keys of truth were dangerous and could only be handled by the king or the priests, but before his death, Christopher announced that there were more keys of truth available and all had the ability to set people free.

"Beware of those who try to control the keys of truth," he shouted from the gallows. "Those who control the truth you hear, control you."

It is said that a curse fell on the king and the priests after Christopher's death. While their hands remained free, their hearts became shackled. They lived in constant fear that more keys would be found, and they lived with the constant agony of knowing they had bought the keys of truth with lies.

the Dysmorphian Curse

Bonus

From John's next book

"Childlike"

The Dysmorphian Curse

Once upon a time, in a faraway land, three fairies appeared in the throne room of a great king. Such appearances were very rare. Most did not believe fairies existed. The fairies told the astonished king that one of his daughters had done them a great boon and they wanted to reward her. They promised that this daughter would grow up to be the most beautiful maiden in the land and, if she married a handsome prince, they would start an empire together that would bring peace and prosperity to all the land.

The king rejoiced, but before he could ask the fairies which of his twelve daughters they spoke of, the fairies disappeared.

The next day, the king spoke with each of his daughters and told them what the fairies had said. He asked each of them if they had done a great boon for the fairies. One by one each denied that she had met any fairies, but when at last he came to his oldest daughter, Latrilla, she lied and said that she had helped a fairy with a broken wing.

The king celebrated with Latrilla, and soon the word spread throughout the land and handsome princes from far and wide traveled to the kingdom to win favor with her.

Latrilla loved the attention she was receiving, but she knew she was not the one of whom the fairies spoke. She began to worry about the sister whom the fairies really had blessed. Finally, one night she traveled secretly to meet with a wicked sorceress who had been banished from her land.

The sorceress told her that she could tell her which of her sisters had been blessed and could perhaps undo the blessing and help Latrilla to rule the kingdom instead, but it would cost a horrible price. Latrilla agreed to allow the sorceress to come back into the kingdom and promised to give the sorceress her firstborn son.

"It is your sister, Shalana," said the sorceress.

"Shalana!" Latrilla said. "It couldn't be."

Shalana was the youngest and wasn't anything like a princess. She liked to play in the woods with animals and seemed far more interested in playing her harp and singing than in learning how to rule a kingdom.

"Shalana rescued a forest animal that was special to the fairies," said the Sorceress. "She will grow to be the most beautiful maiden in the land."

"You must undo the fairies' spell!" demanded Latrilla.

"This cannot be done," said the sorceress. "The fairies' spells are powerful. They cannot be broken. However, I can throw a curse on her that will accomplish the same thing."

"What is it?"

"The Dysmorphian Curse. It will cause her to focus on her flaws so they seem much greater than they are, and it will cause her to be blind to her own beauty."

"How will that help us?"

"No one is perfectly beautiful," replied the sorceress. "The creator gives everyone a few flaws. Shalana shall indeed grow up to be the most beautiful maiden in the land, but, whenever she looks in a mirror she will be blind to all her good features. All she will be able to see will be her imperfections. She will become convinced not that she is the most beautiful maiden in the land, but rather that she is the most ugly maiden in the land."

"I still don't see how that will help," said Latrilla. "Everyone else will still think she's beautiful."

"You don't understand, my child. Beauty is only partly physical. True beauty exists mostly in the mind and heart. If she doesn't believe she is beautiful, she will not be beautiful."

"But there is one catch to this spell," the sorceress said.

"What's that?"

"If a handsome prince kisses her, the curse will be broken."

"If she's that beautiful, it might happen," said Latrilla.

"In all of history, once this spell has been cast, it has never been broken," the Sorceress said. Then with a sly smile, she said, "Trust me." Doing so, she coined a phrase that evil people would use for countless ages after her.

ii

Latrilla's doubts quickly melted away when she saw Shalana scream as she looked in a mirror. The young girl began to hide in her room. She wore baggy clothes that hid her body. She rolled up her long beautiful hair, and hid it beneath a scarf. She always moved to the back of any crowd where no one would see her.

Spotting her sensitivity, her sisters teased her and told her that she was ugly. They knew they could get a reaction from her. This only confirmed Shalana's belief that she was the ugliest girl alive.

As the years passed, Shalana grew more and more beautiful, but few noticed her beauty since she hid herself so well. Eventually she became so beautiful that some couldn't help but notice. A few of the many princes who came to visit her sister commented on how fair she was. This caused Shalana to run from the room in tears. It broke her heart that handsome men would mock her in such a way.

Each time Shalana looked in a mirror she wept and mourned that she would never find a man who would marry her.

One day when she was weeping, a cat brushed against her leg to give her comfort. The cat became her only friend.

She named him Raphael and she spoke with him as though he was someone who could understand. Raphael always listened.

The only things that kept Shalana going were her cat and her harp. Whenever she felt like her heart would break, she would play sad and mournful songs on her harp and somehow it helped to work the bad feelings out of her.

iii

Latrilla began to take more and more control of the kingdom. No one liked her, but she wielded great power and no one dared rise against her. All the princes from neighboring kingdoms wanted to marry her so they could start a great empire. Everyone knew the spell the fairies had cast on her. This gave Latrilla great influence and many gifts from many boyfriends.

Each day in the court, a young minstrel named Castellerus would play his lute and sing at gatherings. Castellerus was so skilled that sometimes he would distract a visiting prince from Latrilla. This prompted Latrilla to remind Castellerus that he was only a servant. To make sure he knew this, she assigned him to cleaning the palace outhouses when he wasn't playing his lute. She instructed him that his job was to play softly and to support her. He was not to draw attention to himself.

Castellerus had worked hard to earn a place in court, while Latrilla had simply been born of the right parents, but this is the way it has always been with musicians and rulers, so Castellerus tried to accept his fate. It was, after all, better than working long hours in the fields and dying young so the royal family could continue to live long, comfortable lives.

Few noticed Castellerus but Raphael, the cat, seemed drawn to his noble spirit and kind heart. Often the cat would curl up by his feet and purr as he played his lute, and often

Castellerus would give him scraps from his meager food rations.

One day, as Castellerus was playing his lute, the most beautiful maiden he had ever seen entered the room. She tried to stay in the back out of sight, but Castellerus couldn't keep his eyes off her. When the king spoke to her, Castellerus suddenly realized that she was one of the kings daughters, and he knew that a servant like him should not even dream of her. He was surprised how timid such a beautiful maiden like Shalana was, and soon he would notice much more about her.

As hard as he tried, Castellerus could not stop thinking about Shalana. He watched her each time she came to a public gathering, which was only when her father mandated it and even then only briefly. He learned that Raphael was her pet.

One evening he finished playing just as Shalana started to leave. Quickly he packed up his lute and followed her. She walked into the forest where many of the animals came to her without fear. Then she took out her harp and began to play. Castellerus hid carefully a good distance away, but when he heard the sad but enchanting music of her harp he wept.

Finally, Shalana left. Castellerus was about to leave himself when suddenly he felt something brush against his ankle. It was Raphael.

Moved by the madness love sometimes brings, Castellerus wrote a short note and attached it to the cat's collar.

Later that night, Shalana discovered the note attached to Raphael's collar.

"Dear Friend," said the note. "I was walking through the forest tonight and I heard the most beautiful harp playing I have ever heard. It moved me to tears, so sad and yet so wonderfully melodious. You must have left before I could find you. I did find this cat and I thought it might belong to you. I just wanted you to know how much I loved what you did. I wish I could hear you again. Sincerely, A Friend."

Castellerus dared not admit that he had seen her or knew who she was. When a commoner dared speak to a member of the nobility without permission it could bring the penalty of death.

Tears fell from Shalana's eyes when she read the letter. It was the first time someone had said something good about her. Who could this stranger be? Perhaps it was a prince from a far-off land, but he didn't mock her because he had not seen her. He had only heard her.

Shalana wrote a brief note of her own and attached it to Raphael's collar.

"Go back to the prince," said Shalana.

She knew how unlikely it was, but perhaps the prince would see the cat, the new note, and the words "To a Friend" written on the outside.

iv

Six days later it was the night of the new moon. It was completely dark. Shalana went back to the same place in the forest. She felt her heart beat quickly, and she chided herself for her excitement. He wouldn't come back.

She took out her harp and began to play. After a moment she felt her heart stop. Someone was playing a lute right along with her. It was beautiful! The most beautiful music she had ever heard.

Finally, she stopped and the lute stopped also.

"Why did you say in your letter we had to meet at night and that I couldn't see you?" asked a voice in the darkness.

"I have my reasons," she said. "Perhaps I am an ugly old sorceress who wants to drink your blood."

"Not even a sorceress could play that well," said Castellerus.

"Nor a sorcer**er**," said Shalana. "I assume you are a handsome prince who has come to see Latrilla. No commoner could play like you have just done."

Castellerus panicked. He couldn't let her know he was a commoner.

"Yes, yes, that is why I am here. But Latrilla is not as beautiful as the stories have it, and she has all the charm of a swamp toad."

Shalana giggled.

"How do you know about swamp toads?" she asked. "Most princes never leave their castles."

"I'm different," said Castellerus, who was becoming increasingly bold with his anonymity. "I used to be one before I was kissed by a beautiful princess."

Shalana giggled again.

"Oh, so you're the one!" said Shalana. "I wondered where you went after we kissed. Typical man, kiss me and then hop away."

Castellerus laughed.

It amazed Shalana how relaxed she felt knowing the prince couldn't see her.

And so it began. The princess and the minstrel talked and played music long into the night, laughing and enjoying each other, but always staying at least ten feet apart as the princess had requested in her letter.

When they finally parted, they agreed to send messages to each other by way of the cat.

Each day Shalana would wait breathlessly for the next note. She always made sure no one was looking when she removed them from Raphael's collar.

The letters were warm and friendly at first, but gradually they became romantic, and even passionate. The man who wrote the letters was full of love. He surpassed her dreams. He understood her and cared about her.

This filled Shalana with feelings...dreams of love...and then the sad realization that they would never be fulfilled because of her ugliness.

Each day she would sneak into the court and study the different princes hoping to catch a glimpse of the one she had met in the dark, but none of them carried a lute. She even studied their hands to see if they had calluses on their fingertips.

Sometimes a minstrel would watch her from a distance, and deep in his heart he wished he were a prince.

v

One day, as she quietly studied the princes, Shalana couldn't help but notice the wonderful music the minstrel was playing. A chill went through her when she realized that he played in a remarkably similar way to the man she had met in the woods. She looked at him and his eyes immediately averted to the floor. But this was ordinary, commoners always did this with royalty. Nevertheless, she stared at Castellerus and noted how handsome he was. And she wondered.

Late that night, as Shalana played her harp, Raphael mewed loudly and walked toward the door of Shalana's room. He didn't want food, so Shalana followed him with her harp in her hand to see what was going on. As they walked out of the castle they moved through a broad meadow toward a copse of trees. As they approached the trees, Shalana could hear music playing. It shocked her that it was one of her own songs... one no one had heard but the prince whom she had met in the forest.

She quietly crept up to the trees. There was a full moon and she could see clearly. She was not surprised to see the handsome minstrel from the castle.

It astonished Castellerus to hear the sound of a harp playing along with him. He stopped at once.

"You've seen me!" he said.

Shalana spoke from behind some bushes, where she could not be seen. "Yes. Why is that such a bad thing? You are very handsome."

"But I'm a commoner," said Castellerus, and suddenly his voice lost the prince-like confidence it previously had.

"You are not a commoner," said Shalana. "Not in your heart."

"Will you have me executed, Shalana?" Castellerus asked.

"How do you know who I am?"

"I have always known. I followed you to the forest that first night."

"Why did you write me all those letters if you knew how ugly I was?" she cried.

"Ugly!?" exclaimed Castellerus, "You're not ugly. You're the most beautiful maiden in the land!"

Shalana began to weep. "How can you mock me like that?" she said, "I believed all the lies you told me. I thought you loved me."

"I do love you," said Castellerus.

Suddenly he walked around the bushes and Shalana covered her face.

"You were so beautiful I couldn't help watching you. That's why I followed you to the forest. When I heard how you played the harp and learned what was in your heart, how could I *not* love you?"

Castellerus grabbed Shalana by the shoulders. "Look at me," he said.

"I don't care if you have me executed," he continued. "I just want you to know I mean it when I tell you I love you."

Shalana dared to glance at his eyes. If he was playing games with her, he was the best actor she'd ever seen.

They kissed. It frightened Shalana at first, but then she felt feelings she'd never felt before. She couldn't stop holding him close and kissing him.

After a long moment, Castellerus took Shalana by the hand and led her to a nearby pond. He made her look into the water at her reflection. He pointed out how big her eyes were. He noted that her hair was beautiful. He pointed out that her sparkling eyes were as enchanting as jewels in firelight. As Shalana looked she was astonished to see things that she had never before noticed.

vi

Everyone noticed a change in Shalana the next day. She dressed differently. Her eyes, which truly were as enchanting as jewels in firelight, did not drop to the floor when she spoke with anyone. She laughed more. She spoke boldly.

As time went on, her sister's many suitors paid Latrilla less and less attention and found themselves strangely attracted to her youngest sister instead. Shalana had no interest in any of them, however. A few observant ones caught her glancing a little more often than normal at a common minstrel.

Finally one day, the Queen Mother and the Crown Prince of the Eastern Kingdom arrived. Latrilla had waited many years for this young prince to come of age. His kingdom was the most powerful of all. If she married him, she would have wealth and power beyond her dreams.

Latrilla silenced the court. "My decision is made," she announced, and the room at once grew silent. "I will marry the young prince from the Eastern Kingdom."

Everyone clapped their hands and smiled politely, as they knew they should.

"Wait a minute," said the young prince. "I don't want to marry you. You're ugly, and you have all the charm of a swamp toad."

The entire court gasped in unison.

"Your youngest sister, Shalana, is much more beautiful than you. I think I'll marry her."

Another gasp arose from the crowd, who immediately cast their gaze to Shalana.

"I don't want to marry him!" said Shalana.

This enraged her father, who insisted that she would marry him whether she wanted to or not. He concluded his command by slapping her in the face.

Castellerus, the minstrel, lunged at the king, shouting that he should let his daughter decide for herself.

He put up quite a fight against the guards, dropping six of them before they finally subdued him. The king ordered that Castellerus should be executed on the spot.

The guards struggled to bend him down so one of them could cut off his head with his sword.

In the moment of silence that followed, all that could be heard were the sobs of Shalana, but suddenly there was a scream from the visiting Queen mother.

"Where did you get this?" she shouted.

For a moment the guards stopped struggling with Castellerus and everyone looked to see what had happened.

All eyes turned to her. A cat had dropped a small ring at her foot and she had picked it up.

"It's mine," said the minstrel. "I take it off when I play. I don't know how the cat got it."

"Where did *you* get it?" the queen cried.

"I was adopted. The people who brought me up said it was from my parents. I wore it around my neck as a child until my hand grew large enough to wear it."

"It is the royal signet ring from my kingdom," said the stunned queen, "There was a rebellion many years ago, when my oldest son was just a babe. They attacked the palace and it looked as though we would all die. I gave my son to a servant, along with this ring, and asked her to run and hide him from the rebels. We never saw either of them again."

The queen looked long and hard at Castellerus. "Dear Lord!" she said, "You are the right age...and...and...you look like my husband. Could it be?"

"Wait!" continued the queen, "my son had a birthmark the shape of a crescent on his chest."

Castellerus opened the top of his tunic, and there was a loud gasp from all those around him.

vii

Obviously, you can guess how this story ends. Castellerus, who really WAS a handsome prince after all, married Shalana, they started an empire and brought peace by making life easier for the poor peasants. They had a great time with their children and a certain cat. Raphael stayed with them most of the time, except for occasional excursions when he went to visit the fairies who had sent him to the kingdom in the first place.

And they all lived happily ever after.

For More of the Wisdom of
John the Methodist
Please Visit

www.MadMystic.Com

Coming soon:
John the Methodist's
"Field Guide to Religious People"

3766786

Made in the USA
Lexington, KY
21 November 2009